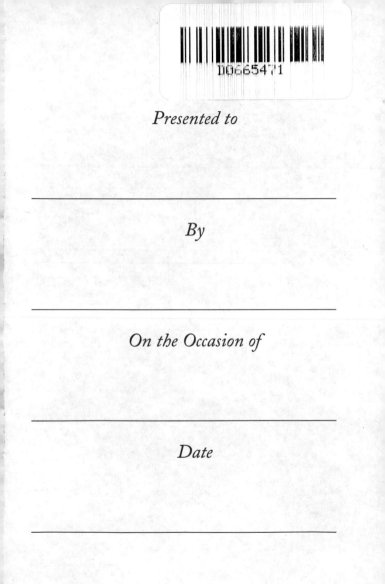

Presented to

_____

By

_____

On the Occasion of

_____

Date

_____

A Scrapbook of Life

A Montage of
Devotional Thoughts

Mary Tatem

BARBOUR BOOKS

An Imprint of Barbour Publishing, Inc.

ISBN 1-58660-569-0

Cover image © PhotoDisc, Inc.

Unless otherwise noted, Scripture quotations are taken from the King James Version of the Bible.

Scripture quotations marked NIV are taken from the HOLY BIBLE: NEW INTERNATIONAL VERSION®. NIV®. Copyright © 1973, 1978, 1984 by International Bible Society. Used by permission of Zondervan Publishing House. All rights reserved.

Published by Barbour Books, an imprint of Barbour Publishing, Inc., P.O. Box 719, Uhrichsville, Ohio 44683, www.barbourbooks.com

Published in association with the literary agency of Janet Kobobel Grant, Books & Such, 4788 Carissa Ave., Santa Rosa, California 95405.

Member of the
Evangelical Christian
Publishers Association

Printed in the United States of America.
5 4 3 2 1

Dedication

To my husband, Roger W. Tatem,
whose encouragement and support undergirds
all my writing. His faith in God's call for me
provides the inspiration which keeps me writing.
Thanks for forty-five joyful years of marriage.
Our scrapbooks are a wonderful record of our life
together and testify of the goodness of God to our lives.

Acknowledgments

I want to thank the many gracious people who shared their scrapbook stories with me. I'd especially like to thank Collin Scott, operator of Picture to Page, Inc., Dawn Brown and Cindy Fowler, Creative Memories consultants, all of whom answered my questions and supplied resources for my research. A large thanks goes to my son, Andrew Tatem, who gave his time and skill to critique the book.

Introduction

Scrapbooks preserve cherished memories, hold life still for a moment, and record our life's journey for those who will follow. Keeping a scrapbook helps us explore the meaning of our lives. We long to find ways to hold on to all that is precious, and to capture treasured experiences. We enjoy the pleasure of creativity and the delight of memories as we record our thoughts in journals, mount our pictures in scrapbooks, and collect sayings that inspire. We feel the sting of life's brevity and want our lives to count beyond the years allotted to us.

Relax with this book a few moments each week and realize how important your life is to God. Scripture says He collects our tears. Even our thoughts are precious in His sight. Discover how He treasures us so much that He made it possible to join Him for all eternity. Instead of holding life still for us, He has glorious plans for our future.

God is the Master Craftsman, planning the "pages" of our lives. He cuts and pastes our life events together for the most pleasing and profitable effect. While reading these pages, give our Creator control over the design of your days and discover the beauty He is able to build from your life.

Out of the Ashes

I thank my God upon every remembrance of you.
PHILIPPIANS 1:3

Moreover I will endeavor that ye may be able after my decease to have these things always in remembrance.
2 PETER 1:15

N othing but wreckage," the man in the black-and-yellow firefighter's slicker grunted, lifting a bucket of concrete chunks. He emptied it into the waiting dump truck. "How long since we found a survivor?"

Shawn didn't answer. He unfolded his handkerchief, trying to find a clean place to wipe his eyes. The swirling, caustic dust that covered the World Trade Center rubble blurred his vision. In his throat was a scream of horror he fought to suppress.

His days were a blur of rubble, anger, and sorrow since the unthinkable occurred on September 11, 2001. The hope of finding survivors in the wreckage of the great twin towers had kept him tearing at the chunks of concrete and shards of glass for days. In time, his hope was replaced by the grim realization that success meant finding fragments of once vibrant people to bring closure to their loved ones. Yet he dug and sorted through the debris with ferocity, determined to clear the land of the scar.

The workers uncovered evidence that God had not forgotten the pain of the survivors. There, in the ruins, a worker discovered boxes of pictures that had survived the carnage. A photo shop at the base of the World Trade Center had been destroyed, but a number of the pictures survived. Dates on the packets revealed they were dropped off for developing as recently as that fateful morning. Somehow the pictures weathered the flames along with the crush of steel and concrete. A pictorial record of some people who worked and died in the towers was intact. At the unexpected sight, Shawn quit pretending and let the tears course down his face.

Tip

Keep negatives of important events in a fireproof box in your home.

Throughout the ages, God has comforted His people and provided His Holy Spirit to console. Isaiah 61:3 gives a promise to those who suffer loss. "To appoint unto them that mourn in Zion, to give unto them beauty for ashes, the oil of joy for mourning, the garment of praise for the spirit of heaviness; that they might be called trees of righteousness, the planting of the Lord, that he might be glorified." The boxes of pictures uncovered after the tragedy of September 11, 2001, remind us that God is always there to exchange our personal sorrow for joy, to plant us in His ways, and to sustain us in the midst of whatever causes us to mourn.

SPIRITUAL SNAPSHOTS

When we turn our traumas over to Him,
He will help us replace painful
memories with treasured ones.

Love Conveyed

Again, the kingdom of heaven is like unto
treasure hid in a field; the which when a
man hath found, he hideth,
and for joy thereof goeth and
selleth all that he hath, and buyeth that field.
MATTHEW 13:44

Latonya stood at the checkout counter of the craft store alternately opening and closing her wallet. "I don't know," she said to her mother standing beside her. "Maybe I shouldn't spend so much money for a scrapbook."

"Are you wanting to put his pictures in it?" The clerk pointed to Latonya's chubby little boy who was chewing on his middle two fingers.

"Yes." Latonya took his fingers out of his mouth. "Anton's barely two. But I could buy him one of those toys he's been begging for with this amount of money."

Anton pulled his fingers loose from his mother and tucked them into his mouth again. "It'll be a long time before he appreciates a scrapbook," Latonya said.

"After all the toys are broken, the scrapbook will show him what his life was like before he was old enough to remember," Anton's grandma said, pulling at his fingers.

"I'll take it." Latonya pushed money toward the clerk who rang up the sale before she could change her mind again.

While Anton took his nap, Latonya began her book with a picture of him in her arms a few hours after his birth. Under the picture, she recorded her feelings of joy about her baby. Over the next year, Latonya faithfully attached pictures and recorded the milestones of Anton's short life.

Tip

Record your emotions about the events in your pictures. They will carry added value as time passes.

Now at age fifteen, Anton often slips up to his room to look at the scrapbook when loneliness overtakes him. He doesn't want anyone to know about his secret tears or his whispered conversations with the pictures of his mother. The book ends with pictures from his third birthday. Shortly after the birthday celebration, Anton's mother died when a tractor-trailer driven by a half-awake driver veered across the median of the highway and crashed into her vehicle.

His grandmother often tells him how his mother almost didn't spend the money to buy the book. He clutches it to him. It is all he has of his mother, and it proves how much she loved him.

SPIRITUAL SNAPSHOTS

We all have cherished possessions.
Many treasures represent sentiments that mean
more than any price we could affix to them.
As Matthew 13 reminds us, the kingdom
of God is a treasure. It is impossible to attach
a monetary value to the joy we experience knowing
God. We treasure the knowledge that
He cares about us and is involved in our lives.
The rewards of maintaining a close relationship
with God are worth any effort it takes.

Well Done

*For the Son of Man is going to come in his Father's glory
with his angels, and then he will reward each person
according to what he has done.*
MATTHEW 16:27 NIV

Look what I found." Bob straightened up from the trunk he was leaning over in the attic. "Boy, this is an oldie." He swept away the dust from the carved wooden book cover. "Franklin Goode" the carving read. "That's my grandfather on my dad's side," he said, gingerly opening the old book.

"Why, it's a scrapbook," Bob's wife, Gina, said as she peered over his shoulder. "Look at those neat old pictures. This one is a tin type."

"I wonder who did all this calligraphy? Take a look at the beautiful handwriting. What a find! All kinds of family stories are recorded here." Bob turned a few pages.

Gina put her hand over Bob's. "Careful, the pages are so brittle, little pieces are breaking off when you turn them. I wonder if your dad knows about this old scrapbook."

"Probably forgot all about it. With his bum hip, I'll bet Dad hasn't been up in his attic for fifteen years or more."

"Which is why you and I are up to our ankles in dust bunnies, clearing it out before we can put up the 'For Sale' sign." Gina shook her shirt and the dust swirled. "This is a true treasure, Bob." She knelt on the floor and carefully lifted a few more pages. "Someone has even drawn little cartoons on some of the pages."

"Hey! I recognize those bulletins. They're from the church Grandpa pastored. I used to doodle on them while he preached. Too bad this scrapbook's too old to handle without damaging it." Bob shook his head in regret. "I don't know how such an old, deteriorated book could be restored to the point anyone could read and enjoy it."

Tip

A spray product is available at scrapbook supply stores to protect old pictures from further deterioration.

"I'll bet I know," Gina said, rocking back on her heels. "The woman who runs the store Pictures to Page will know what to do."

"Boy, if we could fix this book up in time, it would make the perfect seventy-fifth birthday gift for Dad."

With a measure of anxiety, they began the project together. Bob sanded the wooden cover to remove damage from where coffee cups rested years ago. After restaining, he sealed the wood with a spray that prevented the acid in the wood from migrating to the pages. Gina carefully cut out the sections of hand-written journals and stories. She encased them in special plastic before mounting them on new acid-free pages. She traced the cartoons and caricatures that graced the old pages and transferred them around the old pictures now relocated on fresh paper.

The couple was not disappointed by Bob's father's speechless delight. The entire family laughed and marveled over the events revealed in the book. In addition to Bob's enjoyment of his father's childhood, the most unexpected reward was the admiration Bob gained for Grandpa Franklin Goode.

Although Bob's occupation with scribbled doodles while his grandfather preached was normal for a child his age, he didn't have any idea how much depth his grandfather's preaching contained, or how his life had mattered to so many. Little thank-you notes for a favor, snippets from the newspaper about a deed done for the community, and mini-sermons that graced the backs of the church bulletins gave Bob understanding of the strength of his grandfather's spiritual maturity and the extent of his commitment to living like Christ.

It doesn't require a scrapbook to witness to a life well lived. Usually no one records the times when our small actions lighten someone's mood, our caring words lift another's spirit, or our play makes a child giggle. We may not always know when our life revealed God to a lonely or lost soul. But these times are recorded in the heart of God, and the reward for them lives on into eternity.

SPIRITUAL SNAPSHOTS

First Corinthians 3:8 (NIV) promises that
"The man who plants and the man who waters
have one purpose, and each will be
rewarded according to his own labor."
A life lived to serve God and His people,
even in seemingly small ways,
is a life well spent and carries God's reward.

To Good Use

His lord said unto him,
Well done, thou good and faithful servant:
thou hast been faithful over a few things,
I will make thee ruler over many things:
enter thou into the joy of thy lord.
MATTHEW 25:21

"Did you read my Christmas wish list I put on the desk?" Sara asked her husband a month before the holiday.

"Think up another idea. A whole year of magazines about nothing but making scrapbooks sounds like a silly waste of money to me." Tim didn't look up from the desk.

"You watch. You'll love the pages I make using ideas the magazine publishes every month." Suddenly Sara frowned. "You don't think the scrapbooks with our kids' pictures are a waste, do you?"

"Not as long as you keep the expense down. I like to look at family pictures as well as anyone."

To Sara's delight, Tim relented and a one-year subscription to a craft magazine was under the Christmas tree. Her creativity sparked, Sara designed layout after layout that won admiration whenever she went to the local store for a cropping evening. At a "crop party," the women crop their pictures into various shapes with special store-supplied equipment and discard portions of their pictures they don't want. The name is derived from a term used by professional photographers who sometimes "crop" pictures to show only a head and shoulder focus.

Tip

Don't be afraid to experiment when you arrange the elements for your page. Before you secure them to the page, free your imagination to try different approaches.

With her cropping friends cheering her on, Sara submitted four of her striking layouts to the magazine.

Less than a year later, Sara waved a check under Tim's nose. "Look at the result of your 'waste of money.' Two of my layouts were accepted. They'll be in next year's magazine and this," Sara tapped him on the head with her check, "paid for the subscription."

SPIRITUAL SNAPSHOTS

Sara not only used what she learned in her magazine
to earn money, but she also increased her skills.
She was faithful to use the talents God gave her.
When He sees us use the abilities He gives us,
even if we consider them small,
He delights in giving us more and more.
Luke 16:10 explains the principle:
"He that is faithful in that which is least
is faithful also in much."

Stick Together

Not forsaking the assembling of ourselves together,
as the manner of some is; but exhorting one another:
and so much the more, as ye see the day approaching.
HEBREWS 10:25

Azizi adjusted the band of fabric holding his jet-black bangs to his forehead. The material was damp with sweat. Grunting, the little boy put both hands back on his pole, planted his sandaled feet far apart, and threw his weight into stirring the cauldron over the fire.

Tip

Sticky dots available in craft stores are a safe way to attach your pictures in a scrapbook.

"Rashidii, may I stop stirring now?" Azizi called into the tent behind him. "The bones, skin, and sinew have boiled way down like you want, and the mixture is thick and hard to stir."

Rashidii, the servant to an association of Egyptian scribes, took the pole and stirred. "You've done well, Azizi. Your muscles are growing as you stir." Rashidii smiled at the small boy. "The glue is almost ready. Run and tell the scribes to come with their glue pots. I'll keep the glue moving."

Three thousand years before the birth of Christ, Egyptians were making glue. Boiling the parts of animals they did not eat, like the skin and bones, they made a thick substance to bond materials together. Scientists call the protein resulting from this process collagen. By the 1930s synthetic glues called adhesives were developed. These didn't come from animal parts.

SPIRITUAL SNAPSHOTS

Without the invention of glue, adhesives,
and modern sticky paper, we wouldn't have
the ability to attach all kinds of materials
together and create lovely scrapbooks.
Like adhesives, we need to stick together with
our fellow believers in a church body.
When we come together for worship and fellowship
with other Christians, we learn and grow.
By regularly gathering with our church family,
we protect ourselves from drying out and
taking a detour in our spiritual walk.
When an item becomes detached from a
scrapbook page, it's more likely to get lost.

When we aren't attached to a church and
participating in church life, we are more prone
to lose our enthusiasm for God
and drift into ways that are contrary to His will.
There's safety and joy in fitting into the life
and worship of a good church.

Daisy Evidence

Blessed be God, even the Father of our Lord Jesus Christ,
the Father of mercies, and the God of all comfort.
2 Corinthians 1:3

Have mercy upon me, O God, according to thy
lovingkindness: according unto the multitude of thy
tender mercies blot out my transgressions.
PSALM 51:1

Jared stared out the window of his car. The crack snaking its way across the windshield mocked him. If he couldn't get hired for a job, how could he replace the glass before the state auto inspection? Even with his eyes closed, Jared could see Mr. Mandaley frowning in his office.

Jared banged the dashboard with his fist. He never did anything right. How could he have knocked over the water glass on Mr. Mandaley's desk before the interview even began! Now he'd never get a summer job at the factory. He dreaded going home. Mother would ask him how the interview went. He hated to tell her he'd blundered again. Mother could list his long history of blunders.

To his relief, Mother wasn't home. He had time to get a snack before he barricaded himself in his room. When he set the milk on the kitchen table, he saw his mom's new scrapbook on the table. A stack of pictures and a pair of scissors rested next to it. He idly looked at the pages his mom had finished as he munched on cookies.

Tip

To preserve the memory of a gift of fresh flowers, take a close-up picture. When the flowers have disintegrated to dust, the photo of them is still enjoyable.

Wondering why there was a bulge in the middle of the book, he turned to it. "Why did Mom put this old, smashed daisy in here?" Jared asked out loud. Under it, his mother's handwriting told how pleased she was when Jared gave it to her for her birthday.

Jared sat down, remembering. He was surprised to read she was happy about the flower. He thought she was mad at him for picking the neighbor's daisy. He still remembered how shocked he'd been when she scolded him. He thought he was bringing her something that would make her glad. He remembered the sense of failure when she told him he was never,

ever again to pick flowers in the field next to his house. It belonged to the neighbor.

But Mother couldn't have been mad if she put his gift in her scrapbook, could she? He felt giddy from a sense of exoneration. She liked his gift. She didn't hold his misdeed against him. Jared thought for a moment. Maybe even Mr. Mandaley would show mercy to a clumsy teenager. And if not, what did it matter if Mr. Mandaley hired him? He'd find a job somewhere.

Until he was a grown man, Jared never told anybody how his life turned around after finding his gift to his mother preserved in her scrapbook. He explained to his kids how his discovery that day released him from feeling that he could never please anyone. He had pleased his mother enough for her to press and mount his flower even if he had picked it from the wrong place. Funny how a dried-out flower provided evidence of his mother's love for him.

SPIRITUAL SNAPSHOTS

When we grasp the mercy God extends to us, our self-image changes. He doesn't hold mistakes against us. We are allowed to start with a new page every morning. He accepts our tokens of love and our gifts of praise to Him no matter how imperfect we are, and no matter how small our efforts.

Commonplace

Pleasant words are as an honeycomb,
sweet to the soul, and health to the bones.
PROVERBS 16:24

More to be desired are they than gold,
yea, than much fine gold:
sweeter also than honey and the honeycomb.
PSALM 19:10

Celina giggled as she read her mother's common-place book. " 'Sweetest love, I do not go.' Did Father really write that?"

"Well, no. It's a poem by John Donne, but your father copied it for me on fine linen paper. I thought it so romantic that I pasted it in my commonplace book." Violet put her hands on her hips. "Don't laugh at my scraps or I won't let you see my other commonplace book."

Violet then opened a large wooden trunk in the corner. "After I was married I began another book. I copy things I read that sound particularly lovely to me. I wrote a whole page of my thoughts after you were born." After handing the book to Celina, she stirred the stew and pulled a three-legged stool close to the window in order to look at the book in better light.

"Who drew these sketches of pretty dresses in your book?" Eight-year-old Celina was glad for the excuse to stop her knitting.

"Before I was married, I'd go home after church and draw the pretty dresses the women wore. I don't have time for that now, but I still like to capture on paper the words people say. I try to remember ones I think meaningful. When Pastor Benedict says poignant things from the pulpit, I record what he said in my book." Violet got up and poured milk into her butter churn and began to turn the paddle.

Celina knew churning was her job, but she read some more of her mother's writing. "Whose lock of hair is in your book? It's the wrong color to be yours."

Violet blushed. "I put in a lock of your father's hair when we were courting. It was a lovely chestnut color before he grayed. I saved a lock of each child's hair in my book, too."

"Brother said even in 1706 people kept commonplace books. Rex wants to ask Auntie if she knows the location of the one our distant relative, John Locke, kept. Brother wants to see it."

Carrying firewood, Rex arrived in time to hear the last part of his sister's conversation. "Start Celina on her own commonplace book, Mother. Maybe she'll stop pestering me to draw in mine. The other day I caught her just before she drew a design around the picture of the king pasted on the first page. Let her cut scraps for her own book." Rex dropped the wood on the hearth.

"Good idea, Rex. I have pictures of the British royal court. Celina, would you enjoy cutting scraps from them?" Violet beckoned Celina to the churn. "I'm glad the printing press gives us a wider range of what we can put in our commonplace books."

"Why are the books called commonplace?" With a sigh, Celina put down the book and took the long churning pole and began to turn it.

Tip

By photocopying magazine or newspaper clippings onto acid-free paper, your keepsake will last longer and acid won't contaminate your book.

"I guess it's because nothing on one page needs to relate to anything else in the book. We can record our common thoughts and interests in whatever order they occur to us. It's a place to enter whatever you want to remember, whatever's important to you. Organization doesn't matter. A commonplace book is a reflection of you."

SPIRITUAL SNAPSHOTS

Commonplace books were a popular pastime
in the sixteenth and seventeenth centuries,
especially in England. After the invention of
the printing press by Johann Gutenberg in 1450,
printed items became available to more people.
People referred to whatever they cut and pasted
as "scraps." Elegant calendars, too beautiful to throw
away, and poems cut from newspapers joined with
handwritten entries to reflect the personality of the
book's owner. The desire to remember important
events or record poignant thoughts inspired the
keeping of many journals and scrapbooks.
Even more important than what people have said
or thought is what the Holy Bible says.
The words in this Book are not commonplace.
They are the inspired Word of God.
They mold our character and protect us
from mistakes. If we study the Bible,
our lives come to reflect its standard.

Throw It in the Dumpster

Fear thou not; for I am with thee: be not dismayed;
for I am thy God: I will strengthen thee; yea,
I will help thee; yea, I will uphold thee with
the right hand of my righteousness.
ISAIAH 41:10

For whosoever shall call upon the name
of the Lord shall be saved.
Romans 10:13

"I'm getting rid of my seizures today," Holly told the nurse who took her blood pressure. While Holly's eyes glittered with anticipation, her parents' eyes were heavy with dread. Her mother and father huddled together at the end of her hospital bed.

"Hold still, Holly. I need a good reading on your blood pressure." The nurse tried to persuade the exuberant child to lie back on the pillow.

Helen and Jim McCoy squeezed each other's hands, worrying about giving their consent for drastic brain surgery. Their daughter bounced up and down in eager expectation.

"Take my picture with the nurse," Holly requested. "Take pictures of my hair before she shaves it. I want to make a big scrapbook about my 'goodbye-seizure operation.' "

"What will the operation do to her bubbly personality?" Helen whispered as she dutifully snapped a picture.

"I can't help think-ing it's a mistake to allow the surgeon to cut out half her brain." Jim's face twisted in agony at the thought.

"I'm so scared," Helen said as she backed away so Holly wouldn't hear her.

"I know the doctor said the left side of the brain would take over the roles of the right side, but I find that hard to believe," Jim

Tip

Don't feel compelled to include out of focus, over-, or underexposed pictures in your album. You may throw them away.

muttered while Holly giggled about the stethoscope tickling. For nine years Holly's seizures dominated the McCoy household before her doctor suggested an operation to free the child from a life of torment.

The nurse finished and tried to reassure the parents. "I know surgery to remove half the brain seems like a radical step, but I've watched case after case with wonderful results."

Holly's parents paced and prayed during the long hours of surgery.

"I've been saying the Bible verse about not being dismayed, but to call on the Lord and He shall save." Helen wrung her hands. "I can't help it. I am dismayed. Inside I feel like I'm not calling to God, but I'm more like yelling at Him to save our little girl's life and her personality."

Relief that the operation went well helped the parents remember to please their daughter by taking pictures throughout her recovery. When Holly finally left the hospital, she demonstrated her irrepressible enthusiasm.

"My seizures are in the Dumpster," Holly called to every person she passed as the nurse wheeled her to the car. "My seizures are gone with the trash." By the time she reached the exit, a large entourage of medical staff had gathered to wish her well. "My Seizures Are in the Dumpster" became the title of her scrapbook.

SPIRITUAL SNAPSHOTS

"Cast thy burden upon the LORD,
and he shall sustain thee: he shall never suffer
the righteous to be moved" (Psalm 55:22).
We experience times when God is our only hope.
Ask God to give you the trust of a little child.
Ask Him to help you trust that He can take
your problems, handicaps, and grief and relieve
you of your burdens as surely as if He threw them
in a Dumpster. His skill in ordering our lives
is better than the greatest surgeon's.

Silent Witness

So shall my word be that goeth forth out of my mouth:
it shall not return unto me void,
but it shall accomplish that which I please,
and it shall prosper in the thing whereto I sent it.
ISAIAH 55:11

A my, our friendship will be over if you keep talking to me about God. I'm content with my life. I love being with you, but we can't talk about your religion."

One look at the determined set of Janice Bernard's mouth and Amy fell quiet, silently praying how she should respond.

Those words still rang in Amy's ears months later. In fact, she thought about them every time she worked on her scrapbook and mounted pictures that included some of the friends' activities together. Since their kids played team sports together, the Bernard family appeared in her scrapbook often. Janice always asked to see Amy's latest pictures.

Amy shook the ink in her calligraphy pen as she stared at the picture of her Sammy, dripping wet from falling overboard when the team went on a picnic at the park and rented rowboats.

Why didn't I think of it before? Amy chuckled out loud. With a flourish, she copied part of a Bible verse from her morning reading under the soaked Sammy. "And immediately Jesus stretched forth his hand, and caught him. Matthew 14:31."

"Janice can't complain about my scrapbook journaling violating our friendship." In her excitement, Amy spoke out loud. "She knows good and well that we were all scared to death when Sammy fell into the river and he didn't know how to swim." The canary chirped in his cage. "And the current was powerful," Amy said out loud to the bird.

She shuddered, remembering. She still thanked God for the quick-thinking coach in the rowboat behind them, who fished Sammy out before the rushing water swept him away. The coach performed the rescue, but God made it succeed.

One by one she found appropriate Scriptures for the pictures in her book. The ideas came quickly. Her family tried to make God a part of everything they did. By the time she needed to leave for the team practice, she had written a silent witness beneath most of the pictures.

"Oh good, you brought your scrapbook," Janice greeted Amy as they climbed up the bleachers to watch their eight-year-old boys play soccer. Four-year-old Sammy ran his trucks in the dirt underneath where they sat.

"Look at our boys guzzling Gatorade." Janice laughed at the snapshot showing the boys' jerseys stained bright orange, the liquid running down their chins. The caption read, "Summer sun equals big thirst. 'Ho, every one that thirsteth, come ye to the waters.' Isaiah 55:1."

"Does the Bible really say that?" Janice asked.

"Yeah, and later on it says God will satisfy our thirst," Amy said as she watched her friend's face.

> **Tip**
>
> When writing under your pictures, always use a pen with ink that will not eat away at the pages of your scrapbook.

"There's still orange on my boy's jersey," Janice said, turning the page. "What a fright Sammy gave us!" Janice pointed to the picture of the drenched boy. "I'm surprised you could take a focused picture that day. I was so scared, my hands were shaking."

"Mine, too. I gave the camera to another mom to take the picture."

Janice didn't say anything, but Amy saw her reading the Scripture about Jesus and His outstretched hand a second time. They both knew immediate action saved the boy.

Amy watched her friend read each caption as she flipped the pages. She smiled. Without needing to say anything unless she was asked, her dear friend was absorbing the silent witness of God in the life of her family. Maybe her scrapbook with its Bible verses could build a hunger in her friend to know God. She thought about God's promise that His Word will accomplish His purposes. One purpose she knew. God wants people to know Him and understand His love.

SPIRITUAL SNAPSHOTS

God wants every part of our lives
to center around our relationship with Him.
When we study the Scriptures,
we increase our ability to bring others
to know God and submit to Him.
Isaiah 55:11 (NIV) reads,
"So is my word that goes out from my mouth:
It will not return to me empty,
but will accomplish what I desire and achieve
the purpose for which I sent it."
His Word brings people to know Him.
Even our scrapbooks can reflect
our love for God's Word.

Hold Me

Whither shall I go from thy spirit?
or whither shall I flee from thy presence?
If I ascend up into heaven, thou art there:
if I make my bed in hell, behold, thou art there.
If I take the wings of the morning,
and dwell in the uttermost parts of the sea;
Even there shall thy hand lead me,
and thy right hand shall hold me.
PSALM 139:7–10

Good idea to get together. I'll see what I have in my attic," Ruth said as she cradled the phone on her shoulder while she wrote a message on her calendar. "I'll check Mother's attic, too. She probably has some pictures stashed away."

On the designated day, Megan's three aunts gathered around Ruth's table to put together a scrapbook in honor of their niece's graduation from college. The graduation, which had been delayed first by Megan's wedding and then her pregnancy, needed to be remembered in a special way. "A fancy scrapbook is the perfect present for Megan's college graduation.

I'm glad her baby didn't arrive until she'd finished her classes." Then they laughed over Megan's cute baby pictures and discussed how much she looked like her own newborn child.

On graduation day they arrived at Megan's house early to present their gift. Aunt Ruth had volunteered to baby-sit during the ceremony.

"Look at that black hair and those long fingers. I believe she's going to look like her mother." Aunt Ruth peered over her niece's shoulder at Megan's newborn daughter.

"Do you remember what I looked like when I was a baby?" Megan asked.

"Of course! We thought you were pretty enough to advertise baby food."

"I've never seen a baby picture of myself."

"You haven't?" The three aunts exchanged glances. "Why not? There were plenty taken." Almost reverently, Aunt Ruth placed the gift-wrapped present on the coffee table in front of Megan.

"I guess with Mother dying when I was so young, and Dad remarrying, and all the moving our family did, I suppose the pictures got lost."

"Don't open your present until I put this stew in the oven to stay warm." Aunt Ruth hurried through the kitchen door.

"Here's the celebration cake," Aunt Emma said as she set a rose-encrusted confection on the dining room table and hastened back to sit close to Megan.

With their gift taking on unsuspected significance, they could hardly contain themselves. "Let's not wait until after the ceremony," Aunt Emma said.

"Open it now," Aunt Laura urged.

Megan tore off the paper and squealed with delight at the first page. There she was in the buff, kicking her feet on a white fuzzy blanket. Her hair was dark, just like baby Jody's.

"We thought about leaving that out," Aunt Laura said, looking relieved at her niece's reaction. "Most adults are embarrassed by some pictures our parents thought they had to take."

Tip

Protector covers placed over scrapbook pages prevent the oil from our hands getting on the pictures.

"Most people know what they looked like as a baby. Now I know what *all* of me looked like as a baby!" Megan chuckled.

It was the next page that brought the tears. The aunts had pasted together a collage of baby pictures of Megan with her mother—Megan on her mother's shoulder, cuddled on her mother's lap, and curling her hand around her mother's finger.

"This is what my mother looked like?" Megan leaned close to the page. "I don't remember."

"We had no idea." Aunt Ruth stuffed a tissue in Megan's hand. "Don't drip on the pictures."

"She's so pretty, and she's dark like me. Now Jody can know what her grandmother looked like." Megan paused, placing her hand over her mouth. "Look there.

She's cuddling me. I don't remember her holding me, ever."

The aunts converged on the tissue box.

"Here, she's holding my hand. Now I feel connected with my mother, just like Jody and I are connected."

"We didn't know you had never seen pictures. We just stumbled on the idea of a scrapbook." Aunt Ruth sniffled.

"You stumbled on the perfect gift. I don't remember anything about my mother. I was too young when she died. The best part is seeing my mother holding me. Without knowing it, I missed her touches."

"We've ruined your makeup," Aunt Emma said as she dabbed Megan's cheeks.

Megan laughed, looking up at her aunts. "You need a touch-up yourselves. Thanks for always being here for me."

SPIRITUAL SNAPSHOTS

It doesn't matter if we knew God or not.
He was there when we were conceived,
and He was there when we were born.
He holds our hand as we walk through life,
and He never lets us go.
"My soul followeth hard after thee:
thy right hand upholdeth me" (Psalm 63:8).

A Tiny Hole

But now hath God set the members every one
of them in the body, as it hath pleased him.
1 Corinthians 12:18

"Come look at an amazing sight," Doran called across the atrium to his friend, Alexis, who carried an armload of scrolls from a classroom.

Alexis hiked his toga up and hurried over to where Doran stood, nearly bumping into the figure beside him. The man was bent over with one eye pressed against the wall.

"A phenomenon," the man in the white toga said, straightening up.

"Ex–excuse me, sir," Alexis stammered, recognizing the revered Greek philosopher Aristotle.

Indicating a tiny hole in the wall with a wave of his hand, the great thinker moved aside in order to let the light come in. A thin ray of sunlight penetrated the hole and fell upon a small marble statue, projecting an upside-down replica of the statue's form onto the white wall across the atrium.

"It's upside down." Alexis stared at the shadowy

image on the wall.

"Surprising, is it not?" Doran said, staring at Aristotle. "You have made a remarkable discovery, sir."

"How will your insight prove useful in the future?" Alexis raised a puzzled eyebrow.

One breakthrough sparks the imagination of another. No one can tell what today's discovery will lead to someday.

In 1500, as a result of the principle Aristotle uncovered, the first primitive camera was created. An inventor built a huge box, large enough for a person to fit inside. A small opening allowed light to make an image of whatever was in the box appear on the opposite wall of the container.

Tip

Record your children's accomplishments with snapshots. The pictures will remind them that effort brings rewards and is worthwhile.

"Stay motionless a little longer," the Italian artist pleaded with Dominic. The young man's muscles had begun to ache from holding the discus behind his back as if he were winding up to throw it in the arena. As fast as he could, the artist traced Dominic's outline cast on the wall.

"I can't keep the pose," Dominic muttered, feeling the sweat drip off his chin and roll down his bare chest.

He dropped the discus with a loud clatter. Neither man had any idea how the continuing innovations by many people over centuries would lead to the modern camera. Instead of laboriously tracing silhouettes, modern cameras capture scenes in milliseconds.

SPIRITUAL SNAPSHOTS

Although a man or woman's work may seem
unimportant by itself, every accomplishment
builds on the achievements of others.
No matter how small or how personal,
one discovery leads to greater knowledge.
And no matter how meager or insignificant
it may seem when a person displays some aspect
of the traits God desires,
that person contributes to building up others.
Unconsciously, people use others as a mold
for their lives. As we live our lives,
we may only see a glimmer of the importance
of our tasks or behavior.
But when we arrive in heaven,
we will see the eternal significance of
our deeds and qualities on earth.
God has particular purposes for us to fulfill on earth.

Remember Me

And David said to Solomon his son,
Be strong and of good courage, and do it: fear not,
nor be dismayed: for the LORD God, even my God,
will be with thee; he will not fail thee, nor forsake thee,
until thou hast finished all the work for the service
of the house of the LORD.
1 CHRONICLES 28:20

I t's okay," LaVonne said as she dabbed a Kleenex at her eyes and managed her best imitation of a smile.

Joel's chubby feet shoved his walker closer to his mother. His chin quivered but his mouth copied his mother's smile, his eyes intent on her face for a clue as to what emotion he should heed.

LaVonne pushed her scrapbook aside and reached out to lift him onto her lap. Failing, she fell back against her pillows with a groan.

"Does baby Joel want a hug from Momma?" Dora stepped out of the kitchen and assessed the situation in a moment. She picked Joel out of his walker and positioned him on his mother's lap. LaVonne cuddled him against her and rocked back and forth as much to ease her despair over not managing to lift Joel as to comfort her six-month-old baby. His fingers reached for her mouth. Joel giggled when she pretended to eat them.

"Do you want me to clear this scrapbook stuff away?" Dora asked.

"No, I'm determined to finish a book for each child, and I don't know how long I'll feel strong enough. . . ." LaVonne's voice trailed off. "I've done four and there are still two to make."

"May I help you?" Dora picked up a picture of LaVonne fit and tan in her tennis dress, her arm stretched to serve a ball. What a difference between the woman in the picture and the thin woman before her!

"No, I want these books to be a testimony to my children from *me* about how much I love them, and how God has spoken to my heart about His love and goodness to each one of them. No matter what," La-Vonne said as her voice broke. "I want them to know that no matter what happens to me, God has plans for each one of them. He won't forsake them. I want them to be courageous, even in grief, and do what God wants."

When Dora put Joel in his crib for his nap, LaVonne pushed herself up and considered the pictures spread out on her bed. She selected one showing Larry seated beside her, learning how to position his fingers on guitar strings.

She knew how she'd label this one. Every day she prayed often for her eight-year-old Larry. He was the one who seemed to have the most difficulty with her breast cancer. He seemed to vacillate between anger and paralyzing grief. She winced as the door slammed downstairs announcing his arrival home from school. Fury seemed to win too often. If only his natural talent for music could cushion the sorrows of his life.

"Dear God," La-Vonne prayed, "help this book make him know how much his mother loves him. Help me write things in it to help him turn to You and not close You out in anger." She lay back again. While she waited for her children to come into her bedroom, she formulated a plan.

The next day, LaVonne waited until all the five school-age children were off and little Joel was taking his morning nap before calling Dora. "I have a favor to ask of you."

"No! You don't want to do that." Dora's eyes opened wide a moment later. "I simply can't do that, Miss LaVonne. You know I'd do anything for you but not that. Why, what would your children think? I've

> **Tip**
>
> When including three-dimensional items in a scrapbook, use photo mounting sleeves that have adhesive hinges.
>
> The hinges provide a way to attach the sleeve to a page, yet the item can still be removed when desired.

heard them brag about their mother's hair. Long enough to sit on, they say."

"All the more reason." LaVonne wasn't going to back down. "A long lock of my hair in their books will remind them of me, my essence, more than any other keepsake I could provide. Cutting it will demonstrate I would sacrifice anything for them."

Dora was still backing toward the door.

"Come on. I'm not asking for a crew cut. Just cut it shoulder length and that will make nice long locks to tie in these ribbons." LaVonne held up some pink and blue satin streamers.

Dora had reached the doorway.

"Either you do it, or I'll call someone else."

"Okay, okay. Are you sure the kids won't be upset? Miss LaVonne, I hate to cut your crown of glory."

Later, LaVonne said, laughing, "My crown of glory must have been weighing me down." She felt almost lightheaded with most of her chestnut hair tied in six bundles spread over her bed. "I'll write in the kids' books that I wanted them to have a reminder of me. Compared to Jesus and His sacrifice, my haircut is no big deal."

SPIRITUAL SNAPSHOTS

God does not fail His people.
Although life contains heartaches
we do not understand,
God never leaves us alone in our suffering.
A mother, anguished at the prospect of leaving
her young children before they were grown,
searched ahead of time for ways to convey
her love and convey comfort to her family.
God finds ways to comfort us.
More than any human,
He understands the best ways to bring
compassion and comfort into our lives.
Lamentations 3:22 says,
"It is of the LORD's mercies that we are not
consumed, because his compassions fail not."
Even in the darkest place, His love is greater than
the love of a mother for her children.

Progress

In a moment, in the twinkling of an eye,
at the last trump: for the trumpet shall sound,
and the dead shall be raised incorruptible,
and we shall be changed.
1 CORINTHIANS 15:52

"If it's Louis Daguerre requesting it, I suppose I must interrupt my work to cut his copper." Pierre scowled as he set aside his ledger bearing the label '1830s'. He then began to measure a sheet of copper to the size requested by Mr. Daguerre.

"Mr. Daguerre is changing the way we make pictures," explained the inventor's messenger, Johan, as he fidgeted with the brim of his cap while Pierre picked up his metal cutters and began to cut the copper.

"Anything to contribute to progress," Pierre said, his sarcasm escaping Johan.

"Mr. Daguerre can get a good picture with only fifteen to thirty seconds' exposure to light when he coats this copper with silver."

"So fast?" Pierre paused in his snipping to regard the boy, whose face stretched wide with a proud smile.

"What time was required before Mr. Daguerre invented his method?"

"Can you believe it took Joseph Nicéphore Niépce eight years to take a picture showing the view from his window?"

"Why so long?" Pierre allowed a small twitch of amusement to play around the corners of his mouth, watching Johan toss his hat on the counter and throw himself into making motions with his arms that imitated painting.

> **Tip**
>
> If making a scrapbook seems overwhelming and too time consuming, change to a simpler style. Remember, the primary purpose is preserving memories.

"He coated a metal plate with chemicals that were light sensitive. Then he left it in the light of his window until the picture was clear on the metal."

"And your remarkable Mr. Daguerre has a superior process?"

"Oui, he coats the copper with silver."

"Aha! Silver. Then I can expect a generous portion of that precious metal to pay me for my work." Pierre's smile was as broad as if he had stolen Johan's, which disappeared.

"Mr. Daguerre only sent me with these coins."

With a crestfallen face, Johan fished some money from his pocket. "I didn't mean. . . . "

"Never you mind," Pierre said as he selected two of the coins in Johan's outstretched hand and then tossed him his cap. "Remember, old Pierre is contributing to progress." He laughed out loud at the bewildered boy in front of him. "Come again, anytime. You brighten my mood."

SPIRITUAL SNAPSHOTS

Change is not reserved for great inventors and
scientists who make momentous discoveries.
Simply bringing change to another person's
countenance by our words or actions is rewarding.
We can help bring change by spreading the joy
of discovering the Master of Change.
"Therefore if any man be in Christ,
he is a new creature: old things are passed away;
behold, all things are become new"
(2 Corinthians 5:17). Christ makes us new.
Some of His changes take place quickly like
the biblical reference to the twinkling of an eye
(1 Corinthians 15:52) or the flash of a camera in our
story. Some changes require time and a longer
exposure to the light of God's truth like the
photography process of Joseph Nicéphore Niépce.
Our responsibility is to open ourselves to His light
for the changes He desires to work in us.

Insured

Because he hath appointed a day,
in the which he will judge the world in righteousness
by that man whom he hath ordained;
whereof he hath given assurance unto all men,
in that he hath raised him from the dead.
ACTS 17:31

I want you to make a scrapbook for me," Don said as he pulled on his coat and headed for the front door.

"You *what?*" Beth stopped in the middle of handing his lunch bag to him.

"You know. Take a bunch of pictures with our camera and put them in a book like you love to do." Don's grin showed he knew the irony of his request.

"I thought you considered my hobby silly, not to mention a colossal waste of time and—"

"Money," Don finished for her. "I do, or rather, I did. But our new insurance company is asking us to take pictures of all our belongings and put the negatives in a safety deposit box. Since we'll have the pictures, we might as well put them somewhere we won't lose them. In a book, we'll be able to take out pictures of old stuff as we get rid of it. We can add pictures when we buy new things."

"So my hobby's not so dumb after all."

"I never thought it was dumb, honey. I always was glad you kept family pictures in an orderly way. Your books make it easy to look back over our memories. But no stickers, borders, or fancy paper backgrounds for this book. I don't want the insurance agent laughing at my expense."

Tip

When passing on an heirloom, attach a photo of the ancestor who first owned the item.

"Hmm," Beth said, her eyes glittering. "You've laughed plenty at my expense. Maybe a paper with dollar signs for the background and stickers that look like coins would bring the insurance premium down."

"Or increase it because we look like spendthrifts!"

"Do you want me to gather lots of things together in one picture or take individual pictures of each item?"

"The idea is to prove we own these things, and a picture will help show their worth and condition in case of theft or fire. You can click away to your heart's content. Take as many pictures as you want. Just spare me the fancy stuff on the pages. It's strictly for insurance purposes."

"You mean no enhancements."

"Yeah, that."

Don had almost reached the car when Beth realized she was still holding his lunch bag. "Wait!" She waved the bag while she ran down the driveway, trying to avoid splashing her slippers in the puddles left from last night's rain.

"Thanks." Don took the lunch. "This scrapbook stuff has me so flustered I almost forgot to ask you to pray for Paul at work. He's struggling with whether or not he believes in salvation. He's becoming more agitated about what happens after death as he watches his dad's cancer advance. Paul wants the assurance of salvation for his dad, but he's not sure anyone can know they are saved."

"Scripture presents the clear message of salvation. Does he read the Bible?" Then Beth couldn't resist a dig. "God decorates the pages of the Bible with all the benefits of salvation." Her eyes twinkled. "The benefits decorate our lives with joy a little like stickers and borders make a page look attractive."

"Touché." Don leaned over to plant a kiss on her nose. "But no enhancements for the insurance book."

Beth wrinkled her nose. "I'll make up for them with pictures from all kinds of angles."

SPIRITUAL SNAPSHOTS

Sometimes salvation is jokingly called fire insurance.
While salvation does prevent a person
from burning in hell, it is not a joke.
It's a gift bought for us by Jesus Christ on the cross.
The assurance of eternal life through our acceptance
of Jesus as our Savior and Lord brings us benefits
beyond measure. Joy, healing, and guidance are only
some of the blessings that come with salvation.
At the very least, confidence in our salvation
brings us peace. Hebrews 10:22 (NIV) says,
"Let us draw near to God with a sincere heart
in full assurance of faith, having our hearts sprinkled
to cleanse us from a guilty conscience and having
our bodies washed with pure water."

Gain Wisdom

That they may teach the young women to be sober,
to love their husbands, to love their children,
to be discreet, chaste, keepers at home, good,
obedient to their own husbands,
that the word of God be not blasphemed.
TITUS 2:4–5

"What's your favorite memory from your wedding preparations?" Blanche asked, trying to get to know her new daughter-in-law better.

"That's easy," Jill said quickly. "It's the big bridal shower my church gave me."

"You took home quite a haul that night."

"Sure did. We won't need to buy much. It seemed like the presents covered everything needed to start up housekeeping."

"Your friends did a good job decorating the room. Everything including the food was pretty."

"And they took a lot of pictures. Really, the best part of the shower came afterward. Have I shown you the scrapbook my friends made?" Jill didn't wait for an answer but went to the bookcase and pulled out a lovely white album with wedding bells embossed on the front. "I love the memories, but let me show you the neatest thing they did." Jill flipped to the back.

Each page held a picture of Jill standing beside the different shower guests. "I might have worn a solid color dress if I'd known I was going to have my picture taken so many times. Look how my pink floral material screams against Rhonda's orange dress."

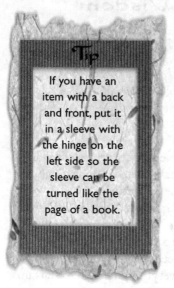

Tip

If you have an item with a back and front, put it in a sleeve with the hinge on the left side so the sleeve can be turned like the page of a book.

An index card rested across the page from each picture. Each one contained a piece of advice guests had written for the bride. The cards were in plastic sleeves so Jill could flip them over to read the backs.

"I'm already using some of the advice these wise women wrote. Look—this one tells me how to keep the refrigerator smelling fresh."

Jill blushed when her mother-in-law stopped to read the one about never being too tired for her husband at night.

"I liked the one you wrote, Mom. Is it okay if I call you Mom?"

"I'd be pleased." Blanche squeezed Jill's hand on top of the scrapbook.

"You wrote that since a man can't read his wife's mind, she needs to tell him plainly what she's thinking. I think I have a tendency to keep too quiet about what's going on in my head. I told Bill you wrote that, and he said we should both do that. So I told him I'd be disappointed if he forgot our first week anniversary, and he looked so funny. He had no idea I was sentimental about silly stuff like that. He remembered, too, and brought me a daffodil."

Blanche could hardly concentrate on the rest of the book because of the joy that flowed over her. God was answering her prayers and allowing her to see into her daughter-in-law's heart. She liked what she saw.

SPIRITUAL SNAPSHOTS

If young women absorb insights about family life
and relationships from older,
more experienced women,
they gain wisdom without needing to experience
some of the trials that contributed
to the older woman's understanding.
Regardless of age, women can learn from others
as Titus 2 recommends.

Press the Button

And Moses said unto the people, Fear ye not,
stand still, and see the salvation of the LORD,
which he will shew to you to day:
for the Egyptians whom ye have seen to day,
ye shall see them again no more for ever.
The LORD shall fight for you,
and ye shall hold your peace.
EXODUS 14:13–14

Everyone, come to the parlor," Kenneth said. He stood at the base of the staircase where he had removed his derby hat and hung it on the newel post. He looked up the gently curving stairs to see his wife step out of the children's nursery. "Bring the children down. I have a surprise." He held up a satchel. He held it higher when Kenny and Belle scrambled down the steps and tried to peek at the surprise. His wife, Julia, followed with Reggie who wiggled in her arms to get down.

In the parlor, Julia put Reggie on the Oriental carpet. With a crablike maneuver, he hitched himself to the red velvet sofa and pulled himself up. Not to be outdone by his siblings, he teetered on the outer sides of his feet toward his father's satchel. Kenneth reached out and steadied him for his last steps. His eyes met Julia's for a moment of shared grief.

"That-a-boy, Reggie. Don't let anything stop you." Kenneth picked him up. "Let's go outside in the sunshine so I can show you our surprise."

Kenneth sat on the lawn, oblivious to the fresh grass stains on his best pinstriped pants. He pulled out a square box.

Tip

Mail-order film processing often offers less expensive developing charges.

"What is it?" Kenny asked.

"A box, can't you see?" Belle spoke with the superiority of a seven year old.

"Ah, but it is much more special than a box," Kenneth said. "Everyone gather together close, and I'll take your picture."

"What's a picture?" Kenny asked.

"A picture is like what you see in a book." Belle looked down at Kenny. "Don't you know anything?"

"This is a camera." Kenneth looked through the lens.

"A camera!" Julia pursed her lips. "Kenneth, I thought we were saving every penny to take Reggie to the specialist in New York City."

"We are. This camera is within our budget."

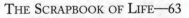

Kenneth aimed the small box. "Everybody look happy."

"Wait," Julia said. "Don't you want a blanket or something to cover Reggie's crippled feet?"

"No," Kenneth said, kneeling for a better angle. "We'll make a record today of what they look like before God does His miracle. We've prayed and asked God to help our boy. Now it's time to trust Him to find a solution for Reggie. George Eastman's new Kodak box camera will help us remember happy moments."

Julia smiled for the picture. She was thankful for Kenneth's strong faith, especially when hers felt weak like Reggie's twisted little feet. God would find a way for Reggie to walk just like He found a way for the Israelites to cross the Red Sea.

"Kenneth, we don't have a darkroom. How are you going to develop your pictures?"

"I won't. I just send the whole camera back to Eastman's plant. They develop the film and make prints, then they put new film in the camera and return it to me. Their slogan is, 'You push the button. We do the rest.' "

"Like what you keep telling me about Reggie. We push the button by praying then we trust God and watch Him do the rest."

"Can I push the button, Daddy?" Belle asked.

"Sure, I'll show you how. This camera is so easy to use that anybody can take pictures."

SPIRITUAL SNAPSHOTS

In 1888 George Eastman produced the first
Kodak box camera. Mass produced,
it was affordable for the amateur photographer.
With the Eastman Company developing the film
and reloading cameras, people enjoyed taking
pictures without having to know a lot about the
process. We enjoy a similar benefit with God.
We don't have to understand how He is going
to solve our problems. We simply send our problems
to Him in prayer, ask Him for His best solutions,
and then leave the results to Him.

Pizza Man

Flee from sexual immorality.
All other sins a man commits are outside his body,
but he who sins sexually sins against his own body.
1 CORINTHIANS 6:18 NIV

"I'm starved," Karen said as she held her scrapbook page at arm's length to assess its effect. "What do you think? Would a few more stickers set it off better or make it look cluttered?"

"Look around this ballroom." Angie waved her arm. "There are at least two hundred women in here snipping and pasting, and every one of them thinks differently about how a page should look. Do whatever you like. And yes, I'm starving. Let's order pizza."

"Can we do that? It's one o'clock in the morning."

"Sure we can. There's an all-night pizza place nearby. The hotel put the phone number by the telephone in the lobby. My dinner's long gone, but I'm on a roll. I'm not stopping to go get food."

"Count me in," Molly said from across the table, picking up her purse. "My stomach's growling."

The table of women appointed Karen to phone in an order. They tried to keep their voices down because they didn't want to take time away from their projects to coordinate an order from twenty-five tables of women.

Relishing a weekend of freedom from responsibilities in a resort hotel and enjoying the constant activity of a scrapbook cropping, no one wanted to go to bed. The more tired the women became, the sillier they grew. Scissors continued to flash, glue sticks rolled from one woman to the next, and the noise level rose while Karen called in the order for her table.

In less than a half hour, a hapless young college man, working the night shift to augment his income, appeared in the paneled double doors to the ballroom. Carrying five pizzas and surveying the room packed with two hundred women, his mind must have reeled at the prospect of finding the person who placed the order. When no one stepped up to claim the boxes, he yelled as loud as he could, "Who ordered the pizzas?"

"We did."

"No, we did, if you come with the pizza."

"This way. Now he's a hunk."

"Wow! Busy, big man?"

"Do you take kisses for pay?"

Glad her table was near the door, Karen rushed over to rescue the young man. While she counted out the money, the women thronged the courier.

"What's your name?" Cameras began to click.

"Jeff," he mumbled, his face as red as the sauce that coated the pizzas.

"Here, someone take my picture with Jeff."

"I want my picture with him next."

"Let's take our whole table with this handsome guy. It'll make the perfect ending for our scrapbooks."

The ballroom was ablaze with flashing cameras. Between hunger pangs, the late hour, and the unusual freedom from responsibilities, the women's silliness escalated to near idiocy.

Tip

Stop for a break before you become so tired you begin to make mistakes in your scrapbook.

"Can you stay? My room number's 270."

"I guess some of them are feeling a little too liberated," Karen apologized.

Jeff hurried to the nearest table and put the boxes down, stuffed Karen's money into his pocket, and bolted from the room, chased by the sound of uproarious laughter.

"Smart young man," Karen said, handing the pizza boxes to the ones at her table. "He knew he needed to flee." Later she added his picture at the end of her album as a reminder that even freedom requires limits.

Spiritual Snapshots

When our guard is down because of fatigue
or loneliness, or simply a giddy sense of freedom
like some of these women experienced,
we are protected if we remember the wisdom
contained in the Scriptures.
"Flee also youthful lusts: but follow righteousness,
faith, charity, peace, with them that call on
the Lord out of a pure heart" (2 Timothy 2:22).
Wise people don't test their ability to
resist sin and still stay close to it.
Wisdom will run from situations that offer
temptation. The young pizza deliverer was astute
not to test his ability to withstand temptation but,
instead, to run from it quickly.

Rekindle

The fig tree putteth forth her green figs,
and the vines with the tender grape give a good smell.
Arise, my love, my fair one, and come away.
O my dove, that art in the clefts of the rock,
in the secret places of the stairs,
let me see thy countenance,
let me hear thy voice; for sweet is thy voice,
and thy countenance is comely.
SONG OF SOLOMON 2:13–14

We don't do anything together anymore. Since the kids left home and we aren't hurrying off to some sport or the other, it seems as if we don't have anything to pull us together." Anne plopped down next to her husband on the sofa and wiggled up under his arm holding the newspaper.

"Looks like we're cuddling to me." Hal put the paper down and squeezed her shoulder.

"Feels good, too." Anne snuggled closer. "But I'd still like us to do something together. We need to share something besides TV shows."

"What do you have up your sleeve? We've been

married so long, I know you are about to pop a togetherness idea."

"Well, I've been thinking about all those snapshots we took when the kids were growing up and just threw into boxes because we were too busy to do anything with them. I think it'd be fun for us to spend time making beautiful scrapbooks for each of the kids."

"I dunno, Anne. You mean all those sticker things and printed papers I see our daughter do? I don't think I could get interested in that."

"Could you at least help me sort pictures and figure out which ones should go in which child's book? You could organize the pictures for each page. Please?" Anne planted a kiss on Hal's chin.

"You need a better aim than that." Hal took her face in his hands.

> **Tip**
>
> Instead of a chronological approach, try making pages that show a particular activity being done over the years. For instance, make a spread beginning with pictures of a boy first playing T-ball and progressing all the way to a high school playoff game.

"We may have an empty nest, but we haven't lost the knack for a real kiss."

Hal enjoyed the memories when they sorted through the boxes of snapshots. During a reluctant visit to the local scrapbook supply store, he surprised himself by enjoying the search for specialty paper and borders and stickers that tied the pages together according to the theme. The couple often spent an entire evening conversing over the dining room table as they prepared their pages. Television became a less dominant part of their evenings and conversation blossomed. To Hal and Anne's delight, the scrapbook projects rekindled their romance.

SPIRITUAL SNAPSHOTS

When the wedding anniversaries add up
and the challenges of life pile high,
couples need to make a conscious
decision to enjoy each other.
A common interest can help couples
rediscover their appreciation for one another.

Adopted

That which we have seen and heard declare we unto you,
that ye also may have fellowship with us:
and truly our fellowship is with the Father,
and with his Son Jesus Christ.
1 JOHN 1:3

L et's include some pictures from our family re-
unions." Kara placed photos on the coffee table.
"These will show we value family."

"Here are some shots taken at the church picnic."
Ben started his own pile. "In this one, you're playing
volleyball. In that one, I'm playing softball. Maybe the
adoption agency will catch the hint we're not only
involved in church, but we know how to have fun."

"Good idea. Let's take pictures next Sunday when
it's our turn to work in the infant nursery. We can
prove we're comfortable with little ones."

"Didn't you think the social worker asked a lot of
questions about our house and neighborhood?" Ben
frowned at the memory. "I couldn't believe all the
personal stuff she asked like how much we spent on
this and that."

"Felt like a police grilling. I never did figure out if we were supposed to look frugal or as if we had plenty of money to meet any need that arises."

"I'm glad you thought up this idea of making a scrapbook to represent our life." Ben made a thumbs-up gesture.

Tip

A gentle sawing motion with dental floss helps remove pictures from old albums.

Ben and Kara's social worker graciously received their pictorial effort to show themselves qualified to adopt a baby. Several months later, after they had received their baby girl, they continued to make scrapbooks to record the milestones in their beautiful daughter's life. Each time the social worker visited, there were new pages to show her. She enjoyed their glimpses of everyday life, and the evidence of love poured on baby Allison filled her with job satisfaction.

SPIRITUAL SNAPSHOTS

We rejoice every time loving parents
adopt a baby and rescue the child
from the instability of institutions.
We know adoption gives the child an opportunity
to achieve emotional stability and mature
into a healthy member of society.
We can rejoice every time a person joins
God's family through receiving Jesus Christ.
We are plucked from the loneliness and isolation
of this world and adopted into the family of
God where we are nourished and given
the emotional stability that only God's love
can provide. "He predestined us to be adopted
as his sons through Jesus Christ,
in accordance with his pleasure and will"
(Ephesians 1:5 NIV).

Move On

And be ye kind one to another, tenderhearted,
forgiving one another,
even as God for Christ's sake hath forgiven you.
EPHESIANS 4:32

Gloria couldn't hide her delight when her relatives praised her watercolor artwork around the edges of the ancestors' portraits in her album. Since many of the pictures were the only copies in existence, her aunts were seeing them for the first time.

"What a lot of work," Grandma said.

"Took me two years, but it's worth it to see your enjoyment."

Satisfied the scrapbook was a hit, she laid the album out with the rest of her luggage for the trip back home to Virginia. Loading the car, Gloria and her husband Alan were frequently interrupted by relatives reluctant to see them leave.

"You did pack the scrapbook, didn't you?" Gloria asked Alan after they had brought the luggage into their living room at home.

"I remember carrying it to the car." Alan was certain.

"But I can't find it."

When everything was put away and the scrapbook hadn't appeared, Gloria glared at her husband. "What did you do with my scrapbook?"

The tense atmosphere didn't improve when they phoned Kansas and pieced together what happened.

Alan had carried the book to the car all right, but he laid it on the roof while he arranged other things. When they drove off, the precious treasure slid off the top of the car and into a ditch about two blocks from the family farm. A thunderstorm and several days in a wet ditch ruined the book. The watercolors bled all over the pictures. The cardboard backing of the pictures was reduced to wet mush.

Gloria's anger at her husband of thirty-four years could not be mollified, and the couple faced a crisis that

> **Tip**
>
> If you make a mistake in your journaling, remember mistakes are a part of your humanity and go on. If you find your entry contains misinformation, cover the section with a piece of paper and begin again.

threatened to destroy their marriage. Gradually, Gloria realized the energy required to keep her wrath festering was better directed at restoring her marriage.

SPIRITUAL SNAPSHOTS

As important as her keepsake was,
Gloria nearly threw away her marriage
for a possession. Possessions never bring more
pleasure and value to our lives than relationships.
To overcome a breach in a relationship,
one must forgive offenses. Christ died a horrible
death to allow us to find forgiveness for our offenses,
both large and small. Picturing His crucifixion gives
us motivation to put away ill will and forgive others.

Beauty

How beautiful upon the mountains are the feet of him
that bringeth good tidings, that publisheth peace;
that bringeth good tidings of good, that publisheth
salvation; that saith unto Zion, Thy God reigneth!
ISAIAH 52:7

Look at these beautiful pictures," Lillian said as she
put down her Limoges teacup to hand an elegant
book to her friend, Eleanor.

"How did you get such wonderful pictures for
your commonplace book?" Eleanor ran her hand over
the marbled binding.

"Beauregard brought these pictures when he was
calling on me." Lillian pointed to a few pages where a
winding river lined with lush green river banks wove
through a village of thatched homes. "He also brought
me these exotic pictures of castle ruins on the Rhine
River." She flipped a few pages over.

"That's when Papa decided Beauregard was too
much into adventure to make a solid family man.
Goodbye, Beauregard, and hello, Percy. Percy's father
doesn't go on adventures. He simply helps fund them."

She directed Eleanor's attention to the next set of pictures, snow scenes taken from France's Mont Blanc, the highest mountain in the Alps located between France and Italy. "Percy's papa told us about Louis Bisson's journey to take these pictures."

Lillian gave such a graphic account that Eleanor formed mental pictures of the event.

In her mind's eye, she could see Louis Bisson lowering his head and hunching his shoulders as he faced the wind. She shut her eyes and let her imagination loose.

Louis drew in a deep breath and then nearly doubled over from the stabbing cold in his lungs. In vain he dug his fingers into his calves each time he leaned forward to make the next step up the steep mountainside. His clothing was too thick for him to massage his straining muscles.

Tip

Make extra copies of friends' and neighbors' pictures and give them freely.

"Bah!" His warm grunt of disgust turned into a puff of steam in the cold air, leaving a skim of moisture over his mustache that promptly turned into ice. Brushing at the crystals with his glove, he scolded himself. Don't exhale any more hot air than your breathing requires.

He looked around at the twenty-five porters carrying his ponderous camera equipment up France's Mont Blanc. The team moved as quietly as possible. Silence was wise.

Not that I have enough breath left for conversation, *Louis thought ruefully. The porters, familiar with the mountain, warned of the danger of avalanches. Louis froze midstep as a menacing crack reverberated through the air. He held his breath. The leader flung his arm up in warning, but the plodding line of men knew the danger and instantly halted as if paralyzed. After assuring himself that the danger was in another location, the porter motioned the column forward, and Louis forced his legs to climb again.* Are the hearts of the others pounding as hard as mine? *Louis wondered when ominous cracks cut through the air time and again.*

With conversation impossible, Louis carried on an inner dialogue with himself. The reward is worth the cost, *Louis reminded himself when his boots sunk thigh deep into the snow. The struggle to move ahead made him pant.*

"Careful," *the porter behind him said, breaking the silence. He stopped Louis's slide as his boots hit a patch of ice.*

The ropes will hold, *he told himself. He goaded himself forward by focusing on the end result.* No one else will make such a difficult trip so my pictures will command high prices.

He was not disappointed. When his caravan reached the summit, the view renewed his enthusiasm. Interrupted only by grunts, he and his porters set up the cumbersome equipment. The pictures he took from the top of Mont Blanc gathered an enthusiastic following from the devotees of photography. The spectacular scenes gleaming with snow, the crags of sheer mountain drops, and the contrast of mountain peaks to snow-encrusted trees in the valleys made a grand reputation for the man.

From 1850 until 1860, eager fans of pictures, like Lillian and Eleanor, began to buy photos and mount them in books to enjoy. During these years, photographers concentrated on taking scenes of landscapes, European historical sites, and the Middle East, where early Christianity unfolded. A man named Nadir reaped rewards by taking the first aerial photo from a balloon floating over Paris.

Although cameras were still large and awkward, they shrank the world. People could see sights they would never see for themselves. Photography revealed the beauty of the world. People began putting pictures in books to pick up and look at again and again.

SPIRITUAL SNAPSHOTS

The beauty of God's world was first
recorded in pictures by adventurers
who traveled to little-known places
and took pictures with equipment
primitive by today's standards.
The Bible tells us that there is beauty
in the feet of those who travel to tell about
the splendid plan God designed that allows us
to live eternally and to enjoy the blessings
God wants for us. Famous evangelists and veteran
missionaries who preach to thousands and touch
whole villages of unreached people are beautiful.

Every bit as lovely are the feet that go next door and
deliver a snapshot of the neighbor's son playing ball,
thus earning the chance to tell the neighbor
about God's plan for humankind.

Sorrow Subdued

Sing to God, sing praise to his name,
extol him who rides on the clouds—his name is
the LORD—and rejoice before him.
PSALM 68:4 NIV

"You loved Prince as much I did," Casey said, slumped against the empty stall that used to house her horse. "Would you write a little something about him?" Casey held out a pad of paper to the stable hand. "Maybe you noticed something no one else did because you took care of him every day. I'm making a scrapbook in memory of my horse." She stopped before her voice cracked.

"I ain't much at writin', Miss Casey. Ask Jed." Zack pointed to another man pitching hay into a stall across the barn. "He writes good, and he misses Prince lots. He was a good horse. Fast, too. Never saw a horse fly across that meadow as fast as old Prince. He beat them other horses to the clover every time. He could sniff out a sugar lump, too. No foolin' him. You know that 'cause you brought 'im one every day."

Casey pulled a pencil from her pocket and wrote

down Zack's words before she crossed over to ask Jed for his memories.

Later, Jessica, Casey's daughter, asked, "Mom, are you sure you're ready to make a scrapbook about Prince?"

Casey blew her nose. "Ignore my red eyes. The scrapbook's helping." She put an envelope in Jessica's hands. "Read the letter from the veterinarian about Prince. More letters keep coming from the arena where we did exhibitions. One's even from the owner of a horse Prince beat in his last race."

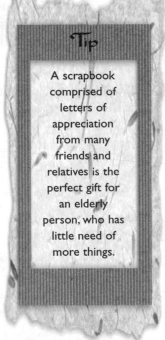

Tip

A scrapbook comprised of letters of appreciation from many friends and relatives is the perfect gift for an elderly person, who has little need of more things.

Mounting pictures of Prince stretching his neck over the finish line, lapping sugar out of Casey's hand, and leaping the jumps on the track comforted Casey. She felt privileged to have owned such a special horse. One particular letter from a friend reminded her of Bible verses depicting God as riding in the heavens, concerned about the welfare of His people—and that included her.

SPIRITUAL SNAPSHOTS

God cares about the sorrows we experience.
He knows how to bring together a montage
of people and events to comfort us.
"There is no one like the God of Jeshurun,
who rides on the heavens to help you and on the
clouds in his majesty" (Deuteronomy 33:26 NIV).

A Grudge

*And I will restore to you the years that the locust
hath eaten, the cankerworm, and the caterpiller, and the
palmerworm, my great army which I sent among you.*
JOEL 2:25

In her dream she was wearing a strange swimsuit
that reached to her knees, while flapping a red towel
at a roaring bonfire on the beach.

Mike stretched when Alicia flung an arm over
him. "What's the matter, honey?" His words were
slurred from sleep. "Dreaming?"

"Nightmare. Hot. Orange and red everywhere
and crackling. Crackling! Hot!" Alicia sat up as her
sleepiness vanished. "It's not a dream, Mike, listen.
Hear the crackling?"

Mike ran to the hall where he saw an orange glow
coming from the den. After punching in 911 on the
cell phone, he grabbed Alicia and they dashed from
their house.

"Looks like arson, sir." Later, when the fire was
subdued, a firefighter showed Mike the remnants of a
can of gasoline. "Do you have any enemies?"

"I do." The couple's next-door neighbor spoke up as he carried a carafe of coffee to Alicia and Mike, already wrapped in his blankets. "I teach at the high school and a couple of hoodlums were furious with me after exams and threatened revenge."

Sorting through the rubbish, Mike tried to find the good in the mistaken identity of his house. "If the delinquents had burned their teacher's house, maybe all his children wouldn't have been able to get out. The fire traveled so fast."

A quick rinse of water prevents water spots.

"But why our house? Look. Here's my scrapbook." Alicia's voice brightened for a minute, then fell again. "What a wet mess. They soaked it good, and now the pictures have water spots all over them. Every sticker is curled up and ruined."

Wanting to comfort his wife, Mike called the craft store. Against her instincts, Alicia followed her consultant's suggestion. She took all the pictures out of the page protectors and then rinsed them under water. The spots disappeared. Her next-door neighbor helped her hang them on a line to dry.

The next morning, the storekeeper arrived with hundreds of stickers. "I know this doesn't bring your lost things back, but I thought redoing your scrapbook would help cheer you up while you wait for the insurance settlement."

SPIRITUAL SNAPSHOTS

Alicia found comfort in the generosity of the
storekeeper as well as in restoring her memory book.
Whenever crisis burns down our dreams and
expectations, we find comfort in knowing God is
able and willing to restore or redirect our losses.
The spiritual parallel to Alicia rinsing her spotted
pictures is for us to immerse ourselves in praise of
God while we wait to see what form of comfort
He will bring us. We find comfort in
remembering that whatever has been destroyed,
God will work good into our lives out of our losses.

No Regrets

And they built the high places of Baal,
which are in the valley of the son of Hinnom,
to cause their sons and their daughters to pass through
the fire unto Molech; which I commanded them not,
neither came it into my mind,
that they should do this abomination,
to cause Judah to sin.
JEREMIAH 32:35

H ave you shown anyone else this scrapbook?" Renee asked.

"Not yet, I wanted you to be the first to see it. What do you think?" Brad fidgeted with his sweater. "Is it all right to show it to Mom and Dad? How about my birth mom?"

"What made you decide to make this scrapbook?" Renee turned another page.

"Why? Don't you like it?" Brad's face drooped, and he sank down on the couch.

"Like it? Of course I like it. I'm just stunned. I've never known anyone to make such a detailed, loving record of what must cause you regret sometimes."

"Wait a minute—I don't regret being adopted for one second. I thought the pages about my adopted parents make that clear. Why, I would never have had a chance at a stable life without them. They gave me unconditional love."

"I just meant maybe you might regret that your birth mother didn't keep you and raise you."

"I'd regret if my natural mother had aborted me. I mean I would regret it if I weren't dead. I'm sure glad she chose life and not death for me. Did you read the letter I wrote to her on this page?" Brad flipped over a few pages. "See, I thank her for giving me birth and allowing me to grow up in a whole family. Nothing to regret there.

Tip

When including letters that have been written on paper containing acid, be sure to enclose them in envelopes before putting them in the scrapbook.

"I included all the letters I wrote and received searching for my birth mother. Now that was a scary process. I was afraid I wouldn't like her, or she wouldn't like me. I wrote this letter to her before we ever met because I decided what we thought about each other didn't matter. What mattered was she gave me life, and I owe her for that. I like life." Brad took

Renee's hand. "I've been waiting to show you this scrapbook about my birth circumstances before I could ask you something. Renee, will you marry me?"

"You big goofball!" Renee swatted at him with her free hand. "Did you think your adoption mattered to me? This book shows a thoughtful man, searching for his past, who is at peace with his present. I want to build a future with your kind of stability. Not to mention I love you." Renee's kiss conveyed her devotion.

SPIRITUAL SNAPSHOTS

When Brad showed his scrapbook to his
adopted parents and to his birth mother,
they all were glad to see his healthy perspective on
his start in life. They rejoiced, happy that his talents,
intelligence, and compassion would contribute to the
world he lived in. God has a purpose for every life.
However, He is not taken by surprise when a life
is eliminated before it can even begin.
Although His Scriptures make plain that
He grieves over each aborted baby,
His mercy is available to every mother whose
desperation and lack of understanding brings her to
such an irretrievable decision. Asking for forgiveness,
which God freely gives,
washes away the consequences of despair.

Gone

*He that dwelleth in the secret place of the most High
shall abide under the shadow of the Almighty.*
PSALM 91:1

"José!" The neighbors heard Rosa's scream down the block.

"What's wrong?" José ran out of the apartment, his unbuttoned shirt billowing out behind him.

"Our van! Where's our van?"

José looked up and down the street. "Did you park farther down last evening?"

"No, I parked right here." Rosa jabbed her finger toward the pavement. "Look. There's broken glass all over the parking place. Someone's stolen our van."

After jogging down the street to make sure his vehicle wasn't in another location, José called the police.

"How am I going to get to the scrapbook class I teach?" Rosa's eye's widened. "My scrapbook! I put all the special pictures in the van last night. I didn't want to take time to load this morning." She clapped her hands to her cheeks. "I had a hundred dollars' worth of supplies for the class on the back seat."

Rosa could not match José's delight when the van was recovered later in the day. None of her pictures or materials was in it. In spite of her impassioned appeal to the insurance company, the firm refused to cover her loss.

"I can't replace my parents' wedding pictures if you paid me a million dollars." Sobs replaced arguments as Rosa's frustration spilled over to the insurance representative on the telephone. "I don't have the negatives."

"I do, Rosa." José put the telephone quietly back on the hook and cradled Rosa in his arms. "I put the negatives in our safety deposit box when we moved here. Let's thank the Lord for His protection. We can buy more stickers."

Tip

Keep negatives in a safety deposit box.

SPIRITUAL SNAPSHOTS

Jesus is better than a safety deposit box.
He protects those who live in His presence.
"I will say of the LORD,
He is my refuge and my fortress: my God;
in him will I trust" (Psalm 91:2).
Our trust in God is well founded.
His authority and power are complete.
He keeps us in the shadow of His protection.
When we are secure in His love,
He enables us to see Him as a haven even in the
midst of the storms of life—regardless of whether
or not our whims and wishes are satisfied.
Our desires and fears fade in the security
of His shelter.

Don't Dry Out

He turneth the wilderness into a standing water,
and dry ground into watersprings.
PSALM 107:35

Stand fast therefore in the liberty wherewith Christ
hath made us free, and be not entangled again
with the yoke of bondage.
GALATIANS 5:1

D o you think we're almost there?" John gripped the edge of the wagon seat with both hands to balance against the jostling and swerving as they climbed the mountain path.

"Can't tell," Melvin said, holding the reins of the wagon team.

Because of the heavy canvas drapes around the sides of the wagon ahead of them, neither man had a clear view of the mountain trail.

"The women doing all right?" John twisted in his seat to look in the wagon bed behind them. Margaret and Evelyn were talking to the other amateur photographers, eager to see the beautiful view promised at the top of the mountain. Their animated faces didn't betray any fatigue.

"Seems strange for women to go on one of these photography expeditions." John shook his head.

"Mr. Archer thinks the view from the summit is worth the rigors of the trail to the top," Melvin said, trying to sidestep an argument.

"Why can't they just wait to see the picture book Mr. Archer will make from this expedition? They could stay in the comfort of their homes. If you ask me, women are becoming much too pushy."

"John, that's old-fashioned thinking. We're in the last half of the 1800s. Women have as much right to perk up their dry lives as anyone. If they want to enjoy a journey full of new sights and the adventure of making the first pictures ever taken in a particular place, let 'em. We're opening up the world for people who can't afford the time or money to come to our mountain." Melvin, warming to his lecture, was interrupted when Mr. Archer's lead wagon pulled to a stop.

Tip

Craft stores carry a spray that will protect pictures from water damage.

Frederick S. Archer climbed over the wheel and walked back to Melvin and John. "Sorry to travel at such a slow pace, but I don't want to harm my equipment." He motioned to the wagon his horses pulled.

"We'll walk the last couple of yards," he added. "This is close enough to rush back to the darkroom my wagon provides and develop the film before it dries out."

While Margaret and Evelyn chatted with Melvin about the steep cliffs and the stream that formed a blue ribbon at the bottom of the chasm, John watched Mr. Archer. Using a glass plate coated with silver salts and a wet sticky substance, he only needed a few seconds of exposure to the light to make his picture. Mr. Archer brushed John aside to run to his heavily draped wagon.

"I can't risk you disturbing my drapes and letting light in." Frederick stopped John as he tried to follow him into the wagon. "Now, if you please, time is of the essence. These plates must stay wet during the entire process of exposure and development. If the process allowed me time to chat, I wouldn't bother driving this big wagon to the picture site."

SPIRITUAL SNAPSHOTS

In the late 1800s, as men were discovering new ways to record the world around them, people enjoyed buying their pictures of landscapes and mounting them in what were called "commonplace books."
At the same time, American women began to challenge the traditional limitations society

placed on their gender. They wanted freedom to
participate in society beyond the home.
The truth is, true liberty for both genders began
when Christ came to earth. The freedom to go
directly to God without a human advocate is a
precious liberty. The knowledge that God hears us,
forgives us, and receives us into
His Kingdom gives us freedom
from our earthly rules and regulations.
We can approach our God without fear.
The fruit of this freedom is not self-indulgence.
Instead, Galatians 5:22–24 states,
"But the fruit of the Spirit is love, joy, peace,
longsuffering, gentleness, goodness, faith,
meekness, temperance: against such there is no law."
No matter how dry we may feel when we come to
Him, and regardless of our background,
He will develop our image into the likeness of Him.

Neglect

Neglect not the gift that is in thee,
which was given thee by prophecy,
with the laying on of the hands of the presbytery.
1 TIMOTHY 4:14

"What a pretty album! I think I'll buy it." Paula chose one of the scrapbooks her friend was selling at a demonstration party. "I'd better buy a bunch of extra pages, too, because I have tons of pictures I've never put in a book."

"You need an acid-free ink pen, Mom." Paula's daughter, Theresa, added a pen to her pile.

"Don't you think these fluted scissors would make pretty cuts for my background paper?" Paula asked, picking up a pair.

"These oval patterns are nice for cropping your pictures." Theresa stacked them on top.

"I'm going to get several pages of these stickers with a birthday theme and the Christmas ones. I'm sure I'll have a lot of holiday pages with all my grandchildren."

"Do you want page protectors to cover your pages after you're done?" Paula's friend asked, then added them to the stack.

Paula's enthusiasm wasn't daunted by the surprising sum her friend announced she owed. "Preserving our memories is worth the cost."

"Look what I've bought." Paula handed her husband Roy the sack of supplies when she arrived home.

He took her bag, setting it beside the sofa. "First, look what I've done." Roy sat her down in front of the coffee table that was spread with brochures, maps, and price lists. "We're going on a Mediterranean cruise. Since it hasn't sold out, they're offering bargain prices to compensate for our getting ready on the spur of the moment."

Tip

Set up an area where you can leave your scrapbook supplies, ready to use whenever you have a few spare minutes.

"Just how spurred is this moment?" Paula asked.

"Next week. Now that I'm retired, we can take off on a moment's notice."

I guess I'll show him the scrapbook stuff when I get home and use it for the pictures from our cruise, Paula thought and began making lists of what they needed to pack for their trip.

Enjoying his newfound retirement freedom, Roy

proceeded to plan other short and long outings. The sack of scrapbook supplies was tucked in a closet where it still remains. Paula counts herself fortunate if she stuffs her pictures into the pockets of a variety store scrapbook. "We're having a ball," she told her daughter. "Maybe I'll do fancy scrapbooks later. Right now it doesn't suit my lifestyle." She dropped her newest itinerary on her daughter's table before she rushed out the door to prepare for her latest adventure.

SPIRITUAL SNAPSHOTS

Postponing obligations or chores can
create a major sense of guilt.
Do we ever wonder if we are
neglecting the gifts God gives us?
Make time to develop the gifts that will
enable you to perform the role God desires.
A sack of scrapbook material hidden in a closet
is of no consequence. But forgetting God's gifts
deprives the Kingdom of God.
"And he said unto them,
'Is a candle brought to be put under a bushel,
or under a bed? and not to be set on a candlestick?' "
(Mark 4:21).

Savor the Time

*The LORD talked with you face to face
in the mount out of the midst of the fire.*
DEUTERONOMY 5:4

"Dad, can you remember when I got the motorbike for Christmas?" Sally asked over the telephone.

"I'll have to think a bit. Why do you want to know?"

"I'm making a scrapbook about my childhood, and I found a picture of that bike with a big red bow on the handlebars. I want at least to estimate the date."

"You sure were spunky riding that bike. Hair stuffed up in your helmet, couldn't tell you weren't a boy."

Was the gruffness in her dad's voice hiding a hint of emotion? Sally wondered. "I'll never forget how surprised I was that you actually let me have it."

"Your mom and I argued about it. I said I'd rather you got your sense of adventure from riding a bike than from some no-good boy." Even three states away, Sally could picture her dad's grin that accompanied his laugh.

"It worked, too," Sally's dad continued. "You were too wrapped up in that motorbike to pay any attention to boys before you were old enough to sort out the immature ones. You got yourself a good one with Chad."

As the laughter and reminiscing flowed on, Sally adjusted a pillow behind her back and relaxed, delighted to have a lengthy conversation with her dad. With brief holiday calls the standard in her family, Sally gaped at the clock when she hung up the phone and discovered they had talked for two hours. Their conversation had wandered to things never before discussed. She discovered aspects of her dad she had never known. She shook her head, marveling at the time of sharing simple snapshots had unlocked.

The thought of the long talk with her dad brought comfort when Sally's phone carried the news of his death one month later. Her grief was strong, but her regrets were minimal.

SPIRITUAL SNAPSHOTS

Pictures can spark conversation, provide a new
perspective about the past, and deepen relationships.
Because we don't know how long anyone has
on this earth, don't delay expressing love.
Neither should we postpone entering into regular
conversations with God, our heavenly Father.
"And do this, understanding the present time.
The hour has come for you to wake up from your
slumber, because our salvation is nearer now than
when we first believed" (Romans 13:11 NIV).
At best, life on earth is short, and we are wise
to consider how we use the time.

Crop Queen

Being confident of this very thing,
that he which hath begun a good work in you
will perform it until the day of Jesus Christ.
PHILIPPIANS 1:6

"The Queen of Crop has arrived. Make room for her Majesty." Rachel swept her arm in front of her waist and made a deep bow.

"You guys!" Aileen blushed. "Sorry I'm late." She set her briefcase of supplies down at an empty place.

"We saved you a place because we knew you'd come. You never miss, and you'd better not start missing now." Rachel handed her a sheet of stickers. "We need our Crop Queen to give us advice."

"I know my scrapbooks look better because of the Crop Queen's advice." Lisa moved her chair over to make room for Aileen.

Living up to her reputation for excellent work, Aileen began the delicate process of cutting out intricate letters to spell her daughter's name. When she was finished, she set the letters aside and carefully glued the drop-out frame instead of the letters to her scrapbook page. Aileen enjoyed the unusual look she achieved when she spelled her daughter's name by using the spaces left after removing the letters.

"Aileen," Rachel said as she looked over her friend's shoulder, "how does Ashley spell her name?"

"A-S-H-L-E-Y," Aileen recited and then gasped. "Oh no! I left the 'H' out."

"Can't you fix it? It took you forever to cut those letters." Lisa looked nearly as dismayed as Aileen.

"I could probably pry up individual letters, but these hollow letters will break if I try to pull them up." Her sigh could be heard all over the room. "There's nothing to do but start over."

"The Queen of Crop's crown is crooked."

Aileen managed to smile at the volley of quips that came at her expense, but the discouragement from her mistake made her want to give up.

Tip

When a page disappoints you, simply remove the pictures and start over.

"Come on." Rachel handed her another sheet of paper. "You can finish a good page eventually. You always finish what you begin."

SPIRITUAL SNAPSHOTS

We often become discouraged when things
go wrong. Our response to mistakes is
to want to give up. To our great relief,
God does not give up on us when we make mistakes.
He never tires of perfecting our character
and personality. He sees the end result of our lives,
and His love will keep working in us until
He is ready to call us home to heaven.
We can stand firm knowing
He never gives up on us.

Known

But now thus saith the LORD that created thee,
O Jacob, and he that formed thee, O Israel,
Fear not: for I have redeemed thee,
I have called thee by thy name; thou art mine.
ISAIAH 43:1

"Not another cup of coffee!" Christine moaned when her mother picked up the coffee pot and poured a cup for herself and her husband.

"Why are you so jittery? You're more anxious to open the Christmas gifts than when you were a child," Mom chided.

"I want to see you open the gift Rick and I made." Christine looked at her brother.

"Yeah," Rick added, "why don't you carry the coffee into the living room? You can open our gift first so we can end this suspense."

"What could possibly cause all this excitement in two college kids? You're supposed to sleep in at your age."

In a moment, Mr. and Mrs. Worth were more excited than their children.

Christine and Rick had made a scrapbook for their parents. They had sorted through the box of pictures from their childhood and made a two-page spread for each year of their lives, from birth through high school graduations. Rick's pictures were on the left side and Christine's were on the right.

"The perfect present." Mom admired the album's cover picture of the two children holding Easter baskets. "It's a good thing we took this picture before we went to church." Mom's eyes watered. "Rick, you put a hole in the knee of your new pants before we even crossed the parking lot."

"Must have been a nasty hole if it still makes you cry."

Mom landed a playful punch on his arm. "You were the only child carrying flowers to the altar with a ragged knee. You were so cute." Watery eyes overflowed.

Christine stuck a tissue in her mother's hand.

"When did you busy college kids find time to do this?" Dad cleared his throat and brushed his eyes as if something were in them. Christine handed him a tissue.

"You made a mistake here." Dad studied the first spread in the book. "The caption says Rick, but that's you, Christine."

"Are you sure?" Rick leaned in for a closer look. "Babies all look alike."

"Of course, I'm sure. We studied every hair on your head when you born—I mean, when both of you were born. These are two pictures of Christine. I'd know her anywhere."

"You can tell the difference in a tiny newborn picture?" Christine smiled.

SPIRITUAL SNAPSHOTS

Our heavenly Father takes an even greater interest
in us than our parents. He knows us so well
He even keeps track of the hairs on our head.
"But the very hairs of your head are all numbered"
(Matthew 10:30). We don't fool Him by
our outward appearance or actions.
He recognizes us in every facet of our being,
in the deep inner workings of our soul.
We may sometimes feel insignificant knowing
we are merely one among millions of Christians.
Yet the King of the Universe calls us by name.
He knows and cares about everything that touches us.

Victorian Pastime

And it shall come to pass, that whosoever shall call
on the name of the Lord shall be saved.
ACTS 2:21

"Valentines. Alissa, have you nothing but valentines in your scrapbook? How many boys send you cards, anyway?" Lorraine spread out her ruffled skirt, trying to suppress a wave of jealousy.

Alissa's face matched the red color of the hearts in her commonplace book. She watched as her friend turned the pages filled with Cupids and paper doilies. She fanned away the heat of embarrassment with the one her mother gave her from the 1860 State Fair.

"I have other things, too, like dance cards."

"Honestly! Don't you think about anything but fellows?" Lorraine softened her tone at the look on Alissa's face. "Never mind me. I'm just jealous. I don't include dance cards because there are so many blank places on them. I'd put them in, too, if mine were as full of boys' names as yours are." Lorraine tossed the book onto the marble top of a nearby table after finding pages full of napkins from various balls.

"Paper napkins. Alissa, how do you keep a napkin neat enough to put in your scrapbook?" Lorraine put a finger on her chin. "Maybe I'll save my napkin from the last ball in spite of the punch stains. I was so nervous when Scott asked me to dance that I spilled my punch and crumpled the napkin, stuffing the thing into my purse. I thought my hands would never stop shaking."

"See, you're sentimental, too. My brother calls my book sentimental, but that's because guys are embarrassed to act like they feel anything."

"You couldn't accuse Papa's scrapbook of being sentimental." Lorraine shrugged her shoulders. "He collects the paper rings from different brands of cigars. I like to look at the Indian headdress ones, but I guess the buffalo one is my favorite."

"My brother laughs at Mother's book. She keeps tickets and programs from the theater. She has another one full of calling cards people have left in the silver tray on Sunday afternoons."

"The next time you come to my house I'll show you my scrapbook of paper dolls. The dresses are gorgeous." Lorraine felt

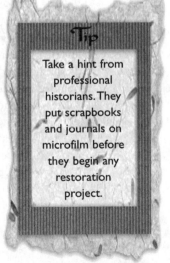

Tip

Take a hint from professional historians. They put scrapbooks and journals on microfilm before they begin any restoration project.

more comfortable talking about paper dolls than courtship tokens.

The advent of printing techniques such as engraving filled Victorian life with paper items people were reluctant to throw away. A variety of paper souvenirs found their way into commonplace books. The term *scraps*, used in England in the sixteenth and seventeenth centuries, led to the Victorian invention of scrapbooks, which became a flourishing hobby.

SPIRITUAL SNAPSHOTS

The enthusiasm to save all manner of trinkets
from our past still drives many scrapbookers.
We save souvenirs because we can't bear to throw
away items that remind us of cherished times.
How glad we feel knowing God
cherishes each one of us!
No aspect of our lives is trivial to Him.
He desires to save us,
not only from the consequences of sin,
but from mistakes and misjudgments.
Each life is a treasure to Him.

Stuck

*But everyone who hears these words of mine
and does not put them into practice is like
a foolish man who built his house on sand.*
MATTHEW 7:26 NIV

Smell the salt air?" Barb rolled down the window of
her Volkswagen Bug.

"Can't wait to take a swim," Carla said as she
stuck her arm out into the sultry air. "Maybe it isn't
such a good idea to have a scrapbook cropping
weekend at the beach. What will our husbands think
when we come home all tanned but carrying blank
scrapbooks?"

"No problem. We swim in the daylight and work
on our scrapbooks at night." Doris pulled a tube of
sunscreen out of her purse.

Barb smiled. What a treat to get away from
responsibilities for a whole weekend and to catch up
on her scrapbook! Just then the SUV in front of her,
loaded with more women from her church, slowed
down. Barb put on the brakes.

"There's the address. We've found the cottage."

Barb turned and pulled up beside the SUV in the sand.

More women tumbled out of the cottage to greet the latecomers. "Sorry we took all the driveway parking." The hostess gestured toward the yard behind her. "We have two more groups coming. Can you pull up a little to make room for them?"

The SUV changed gears and moved forward. As Barb put the Bug into first, its rear wheels began slinging out sand. When she pressed harder on the gas, the tires only spun faster.

"We're stuck!" Barb said with a groan. "I should've known better than to drive this little car onto sand. Now what do I do? I just blindly followed the SUV and wasn't thinking one whit."

"It's predicted to rain tonight. We've got to figure a way to get it out." Doris tucked her sunscreen back in her purse. "I guess a Volkswagen on the sand is no better than the house built on the sand in the Bible!"

"Yeah, and I'm the foolish woman who pulled onto the sand." Barb shook her head. "I can't believe I did that."

"The wise man built on the rock. Guess that won't do us any good. I don't see any rock around here." Carla looked about.

"No, but we have boards." Their hostess pointed to a pile of wood stacked against the side of the carport. "We're going to build a walkway with that lumber. You could back out on the boards if we can get the car up on them in the first place."

"Sure, Amazon women here." Doris flexed her arm muscles. "Just a flick of the wrist and we'll have that car up on boards. Yeah, right!"

The women laughed at Doris's sarcasm.

"You know, we really could. There are fifteen of us and one little old Volkswagen Bug. Come on, let's try."

"You can get a hernia if you want," Carla said, backing away. "A sunburn would be bad enough. If I go home with pulled muscles, my husband will never let me go on a cropping weekend again."

"Come on. If I have to pay a tow truck, my scrapbook cropping days are over, too." Barb pulled a board behind her car.

Doris picked up another one and positioned it behind the left wheel. The spirit of adventure took hold and the women circled the little car.

Tip

Always mount pictures on acid-free paper and use acid-free trims on the page.

"Heave ho," yelled Barb, and they all gave a mighty lift to the back of the car while Barb and Doris shoved the boards under the wheels.

"Look, we've almost got it. One more 'heave ho, the pirates go' and the tires will have good traction on the boards."

Even Carla got into the act this time. The rear tires rested squarely on the boards.

Screwing up her face, Barb eyed the set-up. "How do I back up straight on those boards and not fall off again?"

"How about we pray before you back up?"

"How about we pray, and I do the backing," Carla said. "When I was a teen learning to drive, I had to back up a long driveway that was only two concrete strips separated by grass. These boards aren't much smaller than those strips."

Fervent prayer was easy for Barb who kept seeing a mental picture of her husband's furious face.

Carla took the wheel and slowly backed the car until she reached the road. A loud cheer rewarded her.

"Anybody take a picture of that?" Doris asked. "Sure would make a neat scrapbook page."

"I did." The hostess waved her camera over her head. "Took several. Your red faces and bulging neck muscles will impress your husbands."

"Let's soak our muscles in the ocean before we start on our scrapbooks." Doris pulled out her sunscreen again.

"Don't forget we're here to do scrapbooks," Carla said.

"I'm not going to forget the Bible story about building a house on the rock instead of sand. I'll never drive a Volkswagen on sand again. Thanks, everyone, for rescuing me." Barb blew kisses.

Scrapbook keepers know they must build their pages on good acid-free paper to prevent damage and achieve lasting results. Building our lives on the foundation of Scripture is more important to prevent becoming stuck in damaging decisions and to achieve the lasting results of God's best for our lives.

SPIRITUAL SNAPSHOTS

Matthew 7: 24–25 (NIV) instructs us to listen
to God's Word. "Therefore everyone who hears
these words of mine and puts them into practice is
like a wise man who built his house on the rock.
The rain came down, the streams rose, and the winds
blew and beat against that house; yet it did not fall,
because it had its foundation on the rock."
Jesus is the rock we need as the
foundation of our lives.

A Mended Split

*Remember his marvellous works that he hath done,
his wonders, and the judgments of his mouth.*
1 CHRONICLES 16:12

Tears blurring her vision, Christy accepted the
tissue her daughter, Victoria, held out before she
dumped the next box of pictures on the kitchen table.

"Why make yourself cry by putting together a
scrapbook of Grandma and Grandpa's courtship?
What's the point after their Thanksgiving announce-
ment that they're divorcing?" Vicky studied a picture of
a young couple holding hands.

"That's why. I'm so upset about the divorce, I can't
think about anything else. Somehow putting all these
happy times together in a book is helping me handle
the heartache."

Vicky supplied another tissue. "Better keep going
then. I'd hate to think you'd feel worse than this."

Christy did finish her book using bridal pictures,
pictures of trips, and highlights from her parents'
child-raising years. She wrapped the memory album
in Christmas paper and put it under the tree for what

her parents had declared was the last Christmas gathering of the family under the same roof.

Mr. Jackson moved next to his wife after she opened the gift to look at the pictures. "I remember we tipped our waiter extra because he took this picture." Mr. Jackson sat back with a laugh. "Most money I ever gave for the slowest service we ever had. You looked so pretty in that pink suit."

"If I remember correctly we had to send the suit to the cleaners because the waiter drizzled as much salad oil on me as the salad."

"Oh, look. Here's Christy cuddling on your lap." Mr. Jackson turned a page.

"She's partly on your lap, too. Remember how she didn't want to play favorites and would always insist on sitting on both of us?"

> ### Tip
>
> When devastating experiences make looking at certain pictures painful, do not throw the photographs away. Give the pictures to someone who is more removed from the pain and can still enjoy them. For example, children of divorce still enjoy looking at their parents' wedding pictures.

"Yes," said Mr. Jackson, his voice deepening. "We had lots of good times together, didn't we?"

"Lots of good times." The words pushed past the lump in Mrs. Jackson's throat. "Why are we throwing it all away?"

"We don't have to, do we?"

Vicky reached for the tissue box.

The reawakening of memories saved a marriage from the aftermath of a midlife crisis. The Jacksons went for counseling and put their marriage back together. The years of family life were too precious to throw into the garbage dump of discord.

SPIRITUAL SNAPSHOTS

A determination to focus on the good parts of a
relationship may require a conscious act of the will.
With God's help, we can decide to focus
on the best aspects of a relationship and refuse
to allow bad memories to occupy our thoughts.
Thinking of the pleasant times can prevent
us from keeping track of offenses.
God is able to work His wonders
in even the most difficult relationships.
He is a miracle worker.

Mafia

For you know that it was not with perishable things such as silver or gold that you were redeemed from the empty way of life handed down to you from your forefathers.
1 PETER 1:18 NIV

"Why did you put this picture in here?" Al stopped leafing through his wife's scrapbook when he reached the picture of his grandfather talking to two police officers in front of his hamburger shop.

"It's the only picture we have of your grandpa's business."

"This shows more about his business than I want to recall. I was a little kid, but I still remember the day the police came. Right after the reporter took this picture, they cuffed Grandpa and took him downtown for questioning. My buddies and I were shooting marbles on the sidewalk. I thought I'd die of embarrassment." Al shoved the book aside and stood up.

"As I remember the story, he wasn't arrested." Cara tried to pacify her husband.

"Somehow he talked his way out of charges. The

police questioned him about running a numbers racket between hamburger sales. I think the police made some Mafia arrests a few months later. The officers never came back for Grandpa. I was a grown man before I knew that those guys with the wide lapels and slicked back hair were Mafia. After that incident, Grandpa kept on selling hamburgers for the rest of his life."

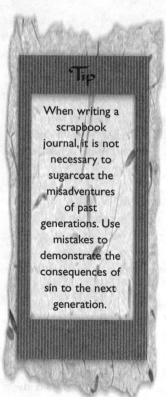

"He didn't go to prison or anything, so what's wrong with putting the picture in our family history?"

"I'll tell you what's wrong. I'm ashamed for the kids to know they have a numbers-running great-grandpa. I don't want them to think our family comes from a bunch of hoodlums."

"Come on, Al. We're all redeemed from the sins of our forefathers and the consequences of sin by our Savior, Jesus. Our boys aren't living empty lives. They are living for God. The picture is a good reminder. God saved them from wrong influences."

SPIRITUAL SNAPSHOTS

Part of the blessing we receive at salvation
is not only forgiveness of sin,
but also a divine heritage that
supersedes our natural one.
In spite of the sin and disease
that may have predominated in our ancestors'
lives, we can ask God to give us His divine nature.
What a relief to know God is able
to remove us from any curses handed down
through the generations!

The Banquet Table

And the king said,
Is there not yet any of the house of Saul,
that I may shew the kindness of God unto him?
And Ziba said unto the king, Jonathan hath yet a son,
which is lame on his feet.
2 SAMUEL 9:3

So Mephibosheth dwelt in Jerusalem:
for he did eat continually at the king's table;
and was lame on both his feet.
2 SAMUEL 9:13

"Good job." Mona smiled at Debbie who held up her scrapbook page for approval. Dozens of angel stickers danced around a snapshot of Debbie holding a little artificial tree loaded with small angels sporting shiny wings.

"I want pictures of you and Daddy standing by our celebration tree when we decorate it with hearts for Valentine's Day," Debbie said.

"Why not put another picture of you in your holiday scrapbook? You can wear your new red dress and stand next to the heart-decorated tree."

"You and Daddy are my best valentines because you never make fun of me about not reading or writing."

Mona held out her arms and Debbie dropped her scrapbook to run into them. "How could we ever make fun of a miracle? That's what you are, you know." Mona patted Debbie's back. "God helped the doctors perform lots of miracles and stop those scary seizures before your fifth birthday. We thank Him for everything you *can* do. Look how well you cut and paste in your scrapbook."

Tip

Sticker binders, available at craft stores, make it easy to organize stickers according to the appropriate holiday.

"I love doing it. And no one seems to care if I crop the pictures a little crooked."

Mona pulled her fourteen year old closer. "I like the way you sing to King Jesus while you do your scrapbook. You're a child of the King, and He loves when you sing your praises to Him. It's like you sit down at the King's banquet table every time you do." Mona picked up a Bible. "Let's read the story of Mephibosheth. He had a disability, but King David made a special point for him to sit at the king's banquet table to eat." Mona was glad Debbie's head was tucked into her shoulder so she couldn't see

Mona's tears. "Just like Mephibosheth was special to David, you're precious to God and to us." Mona spoke over the lump in her throat.

SPIRITUAL SNAPSHOTS

We all bear handicaps,
whether physical or emotional.
It's impossible to grow up without some scars
from life's wounds. Regardless of our limitations,
we are worthy before God, and He wants us to sit
with Him and enjoy His bounty. No impairment
prevents us from moving close to God.

Shock

Defend the poor and fatherless:
do justice to the afflicted and needy.
PSALM 82:3

I t stinks worse," Alfred said. He wrinkled his nose
and tried to breathe through his mouth.

"Yes, indeed, and the stench becomes unbearable
around that corner." Jacob A. Riis motioned toward
a crumbling brick building with broken wooden
crates piled against it. He sidestepped a pile of rotten
pumpkin rinds resting on a mound of kitchen scraps.

"Whooee!" Alfie held his nose, regretting he'd
agreed to spend his school break carrying Mr. Riis's
photography equipment.

"Too bad the camera can't capture the smells
also." Jacob stopped at the sight of two toddlers, sitting on a broken cement threshold, which led to a
cracked door hanging from one hinge. He reached
for the tripod Alfie carried and set up his camera.

"Quickly, Alfie." Jacob stretched his hand out for
a fresh plate to insert in his camera. "Children don't
hold still long."

"Those two look too sick to move much."

"Indeed, they prove my point very well," Jacob said as he snapped several more pictures.

"Prove what? I thought photographers took pictures of beautiful scenery and people dressed up in their best clothes. That little girl hasn't combed her hair in days. And I don't think either one of them has had a bath in a month."

"Precisely." Jacob swung his camera around to catch a shot of an old man picking up a half-eaten apple from the gutter.

"Someone is sleeping in those crates." Alfie stepped closer.

"Correction, Alfie. Someone is living in those crates." Jacob's camera recorded the holes in the shoes underneath the makeshift lean-to.

"Why take all these pictures of poor people in this terrible slum? No one will pay money to buy pictures

> ### Tip
>
> Pictures of children crying or pouting may not seem like what you want to record, but when the child is grown, the photos become an enjoyable record of how the child appeared in different situations.

that make you want to cry and hold your nose."

Alfie watched Jacob's face and with sudden understanding stopped in his tracks. "You can shock people like me who would never come down here and see these pitiful humans. I didn't know such an awful place existed in New York City. Why, it's 1888. I thought we had prosperity in this country."

Jacob A. Riis turned his pictures of New York City into a book. When people saw his photos, they were shocked. Horrified citizens determined to do something about the disgraceful conditions. Reacting to Mr. Riis's pictures, the city abolished one of its worst districts.

SPIRITUAL SNAPSHOTS

Jacob A. Riis proved the saying, "A picture is worth a thousand words," when he photographed the miserable conditions in New York City.
People reacted to the blight he brought to their attention. We can be quick to respond to the misery of people around us, not necessarily spearheading a movement to right a wrong, but simply giving new coats to needy school children. Whether or not a camera ever records our actions, we can intervene with a kind word to the brokenhearted or companionship for the grieving. "And the King shall answer and say unto them, Verily I say unto you, Inasmuch as ye have done it unto one of the least of these my brethren, ye have done it unto me" (Matthew 25:40).

Make it Right

And we know that all things work together
for good to them that love God,
to them who are the called according to his purpose.
ROMANS 8:28

I can't believe I spent $3.75 on one sticker." Madge grimaced. "But I'm not sorry," she added quickly, holding up a five-inch-wide sticker at the store-sponsored cropping session for her friends to see. In the shape of a large bouquet of flowers with the words "Happy Birthday" across the basket, the sticker's colors matched the cake icing and her daughter's dress in her pictures.

"A splurge does you good once in a while," Joy said, admiring Madge's layout. "The sticker makes your page."

"I can't believe I ruined $3.75," Madge groaned a few minutes later. Her friends gathered around to see her disaster.

"The page sucked the sticker right out of my fingers. Look—it's wrinkled and crooked."

"Try to lift it up," Joy suggested.

"Bad move. Now I've torn it. Any other bright ideas?" Madge looked around the table.

"You could buy another one, tear off the wrinkled parts, and patch the torn places with cut outs from the new one."

"Then I'd have a $7.50 sticker! This project is getting more expensive by the minute." Madge studied her page. "I'm going to do it." She shoved her chair back and marched over to the rack where the stickers were sold.

With care she lifted and cut away the wrinkled portions of the sticker and, laying the new one on top, trimmed it to fill in the missing places.

"You can't tell you pieced it," Joy said, admiring Madge's work.

Tip

Use an X-Acto craft knife when doing precise cutting.

"Not unless you count how much you accomplished while I've been over here playing crossword puzzle. Now, I need to figure out how to make it look like that crazy slant was on purpose."

After cropping her pictures at angles she had not planned, she ended up with an attractive page made more unusual by the new tilts.

"Now tell me. In what other store could you splurge and still only spend $7.50? Can't buy a T-shirt in the mall for that." Madge closed her book with satisfaction.

"I'll bring you my next disaster. You've a knack for making them turn out good," Joy said.

SPIRITUAL SNAPSHOTS

God knows the best way to repair
our wrinkled lives and torn places.
When disasters loom in our lives,
we can take comfort in knowing God
is not caught unawares.
He has the power to patch all the components,
bringing the good result He desires.
Our responsibility is to love Him and to seek
His help in fulfilling His purposes.

Left Behind

And straightway he called them:
and they left their father Zebedee in the ship
with the hired servants, and went after him.
MARK 1:20

Marcy stretched, enjoying the sound of her mother clattering pans in the kitchen beneath her bedroom. After her two-year teaching stint in a foreign land, she relished all the sounds and smells of her sabbatical at home. Sitting up, she recognized the aroma of the pungent coffee she had brought from her adopted country. The fragrance set off feelings of homesickness for her faraway home.

"Look, Marcy," her mother said, gesturing toward the television. "Something horrible. . ." She broke off her sentence. They both gasped as the World Trade Center towers crumbled into a smoking mass of rubble before their eyes.

Along with much of the nation, Marcy and her mother spent the next hours following the horrors of September 11, 2001, on television. In the aftermath of the planes flying into the World Trade Center and the

Pentagon, speculation yielded to strong suspicion. Investigation led to military action.

"I know God called me to serve Him in a country hostile to Christianity. Do you think this tragedy will change where God wants me?" Marcy talked over her situation with her pastor after church.

"I can't imagine you could obtain a visa to go back there and teach people about Jesus Christ now." Everyone standing nearby seemed to agree.

Marcy conceded, "I don't need to check the State Department's advisories to know entering this area would not be recommended."

"Oh, Marcy, you only brought out a few things," her friend, Lea, sympathized. "What did you leave behind?"

"The people, the wonderful people," Marcy answered without hesitation.

"What *things* will you miss that you left behind?" Lea pressed.

"I suppose I regret leaving my snapshots. I had lots of pictures of my friends and places where I worked and lived." She shook her head. "But nothing is as important as the people."

"What a pity to leave it all behind!" Lea didn't give up.

"You don't understand. When I left here to go there, I was leaving family and possessions behind to follow God's call. If He doesn't send me back there, then I'll simply start over wherever He wants me." Marcy patted Lea's arm. "Pity those who have yet to hear about Jesus."

SPIRITUAL SNAPSHOTS

When we are willing to leave our physical
possessions and emotional baggage behind,
we enjoy the freedom to do God's bidding wherever
He calls, be it in a foreign country or grocery store
checkout line. When we die, all our possessions are
left behind, but the souls we led to Christ
we will meet in heaven.

High Time

The night is far spent, the day is at hand:
let us therefore cast off the works of darkness,
and let us put on the armour of light.
ROMANS 13:12

"Ray, you won't believe what I found in the back of Aunt Mabel's closet." Ginny left the coat closet to enter the dining room where her brother was sorting the contents of the knick-knack shelf.

"More junk?" Ray wiped his forehead with the back of his hand. "I've never seen so much stuff. Do you think Aunt Mabel would turn over in her grave if we had a garage sale?" He waved his hand toward the table where he had organized rows of china dogs and cats. One end was filled with salt and pepper shakers in every shape imaginable.

"She would already be turning if she knew what I found." Ginny shoved a half-dozen recipe boxes aside and emptied her box.

"Pictures?" Ray rubbed his chin. "Aunt Mabel always said she didn't have any family pictures when I asked her to show me what Mother and the rest of the family looked like when they were young."

"She didn't want to share them." Ginny leafed through the pictures.

"Just like she'd never give you a recipe without leaving out an ingredient. By the way, there are all her recipes." Ray pointed to the recipe boxes. "Be sure to locate the one for her banana cake before we dump them."

"Do you think this little girl could be our mother?" Ginny held up a picture of a little girl holding a teddy bear.

"I don't know. Is it labeled?"

"Nothing's labeled." Ginny turned over picture after picture.

"I wish Aunt Mabel had showed us these while she was still living and we could have asked."

Tip

Send duplicate snapshots to people who are involved in some way in the pictures. Make the gift special by adding a little note of appreciation on the back.

"How do we know who is who?"

"Don't we have a cousin living in Virginia who was in our mother's generation?"

"Yeah, but she's up there in age by now. If we're going to get help from her, we had better not put it off."

A trip halfway across the United States identified some of the pictures. Where memories failed, the cousin provided pictures of children wearing identical clothing, obviously in the same setting. A little detective work furnished intelligent guesses for others, but at least three-fourths of the people in the pictures remained mysteries. The pair returned home satisfied with the results of their journey but frustrated with the failure to identify so many.

"It sure would have been nice if Aunt Mabel shared her treasure while she was living. Showing us pictures would have made her happier than hiding the pictures ever did."

SPIRITUAL SNAPSHOT

Now is the time to bless people. Don't put it off.
Besides sharing family lore with others,
share the spiritual insights you have gained.
A person can learn from another's experience and
avoid some of the difficulties and hard lessons
in his or her own lives. Never delay telling people
of your love and appreciation for them and of
God's love for them. Tomorrow could be too late.

Mexican Food

For I testify unto every man
that heareth the words of the prophecy of this book,
If any man shall add unto these things,
God shall add unto him the plagues
that are written in this book:
And if any man shall take away from
the words of the book of this prophecy,
God shall take away his part out of the book of life,
and out of the holy city,
and from the things which are written
in this book.
REVELATION 22:18–19

"Mama's recipe scrapbook is out again." Margarita pointed to the spiral notebook on the kitchen table.

"Uh-oh, is it open to the awful tortilla sauce?" Juan put down his homework paper to look.

"No, it's open to the sour cream enchilada one she cut out of the Mexican daily newspaper last week."

"I like any kind of enchiladas. In fact, I like most of the special dishes she's made for us since she's been pasting recipes in the notebook—but not that gooey tortilla sauce!" Juan stuck his tongue out.

"Let's cut it out so she can't make it again." Margarita rummaged in the drawer for the scissors.

"She'll notice if we leave a hole in the page."

"She *won't* notice if we tear out the whole page. If she doesn't see it, she won't think to make it."

With a rip, the offensive sauce was eliminated from the Alarnzo family menu.

Tip

It's not necessary to include every picture in your special scrapbook. Use your best ones for your elaborate book, but save the other pictures by slipping them into a second book.

SPIRITUAL SNAPSHOTS

Picking and choosing the foods
we eat allows us variety,
but we lose our foundation
when we try to pick and choose
what we want to accept from the Bible.
Scripture warns us not to add or subtract
from the Bible.
Every part of God's Word accomplishes
something for His people.
If you find a passage you don't like,
ask God to help you understand how to interpret it.
We may need to wait a while before
He gives us His answer;
but when we are ready,
He will show us why the passage
is included in the Holy Canon.

Wonders

Remember his marvellous works that he hath done;
his wonders, and the judgments of his mouth.
PSALM 105:5

D oes a place like this really exist?" Adrienne asked her father, looking up from the book in her lap.

"Matthew Brady says it does," said the distinguished senator, who was seated beside his daughter on the elegant gold velvet sofa. "It's out West, in the Wyoming area. Some call the area Yellowstone because of the color of the rocks there."

"A 170-foot geyser going off every sixty-five minutes!" Adrienne tapped the picture. "I'd like to see a geyser and these bubbling places." She pointed to the next picture. "They look like mother's gravy when she boils it."

"It's beautiful, all right." Adrienne's father retrieved the book of photographs. "Mr. Brady and others brought this collection of pictures to Congress requesting we pass a bill that would designate this a national park to help preserve the spectacular scenery. They fear progress might destroy it with too many "trees cut, buildings erected, and mines dug."

"Vote for the bill, Daddy, and then take me on a trip out West."

"Maybe a bill would encourage safety measures. I wouldn't want my daughter stepping into a hot spring or falling off the edge of a cliff."

"I want to see all the beauty God made. Nothing could be more beautiful than this."

"Nothing but you," said the senator as he hugged his daughter. "The Lord did a wonderful and marvelous work when He made you." He dropped a kiss on the tip of his daughter's nose. "I pray all the time He will water the garden of your life with His springs of joy and waterfalls of delight."

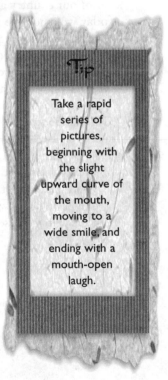

Tip

Take a rapid series of pictures, beginning with the slight upward curve of the mouth, moving to a wide smile, and ending with a mouth-open laugh.

SPIRITUAL SNAPSHOTS

In the late 1800s,
Matthew Brady's photos of the West
and of Yellowstone helped Congress decide to
designate some of the beautiful areas
of our country as national parks.
Today we enjoy the privilege of traveling
to see our magnificent parks.
While we honor God when we appreciate
the wonders of the earth He created,
we must always realize that people are
God's most remarkable creation.
Our scrapbooks help remind us of that.
Isaiah 58:11 (NIV) is a good prayer for our
loved ones. "The LORD will guide you always;
he will satisfy your needs in a sun-scorched land
and will strengthen your frame.
You will be like a well-watered garden,
like a spring whose waters never fail."

Refuse Offense

Great peace have they which love thy law:
and nothing shall offend them.
PSALM 119:165

Did you bring the scrapbook?" Dawn asked Aunt
Maude when she pulled into the campground
parking lot for the family reunion. "I want to look at
the World War II pages again. I can't remember what
medals Uncle Fred won."

"I told my new daughter-in-law that looking at
the family scrapbook is the best part of the reunion,"
Kay chimed in.

"It's the hardest part for me. Do you realize the
Bentley family record book has grown to eight inches
thick?" Aunt Maude put a hand on the small of her
back. "I'm too old and my back's too weak to lift that
heavy thing off the shelf, carry it to the car, and reverse
the process when I get home. Not to mention how
much I feel the responsibility of making sure I don't
mess up when I put in all the wedding, birthday, and
anniversary pictures everybody sends all year long."

"Aunt Maude, we didn't know it was such a burden

to you." Dawn leaned into the car to lift out the object of the older woman's complaints. "Ooh, it *is* heavy. We'll give it to Aunt Suzanne. She'd probably feel honored to be the keeper of the family book."

Before the chicken was devoured, the entire campground knew Aunt Maude was offended. No nephew escaped her lecture about appreciating her years of faithful scrapbook keeping. "Those thoughtless nieces gave the book to Suzanne. Why, of us twelve siblings, she's the youngest!"

Dawn, Kay, and Aunt Suzanne held a hasty conference.

Tip

Use a red-eye remover pen to place a dot of color over a person's eyes where the light has given them a red cast.

"You're right, Aunt Maude, the family scrapbook has become much too large. Since pictures are a grand way to catch up with what happened in each other's lives since last year, the solution is to start a new book. Would you please continue to keep it for us? Aunt Suzanne can carry and store the heavy one." Aunt Maude huffed and scowled, but she accepted the new album they held out. Before the reunion ended, a smile had cracked the lines of her face.

SPIRITUAL SNAPSHOTS

Opportunities abound to take offense.
While we must guard against committing
such slights because of actions, neglect, or idle talk,
how much better to give words or deeds
the best interpretation we can imagine and refuse
to take offense! Loving God's Word and His ways
will help us resist becoming offended.
God wants us to see others through
the filter of His love.

Irreplaceable Memories

My fruit is better than gold, yea, than fine gold;
and my revenue than choice silver.
PROVERBS 8:19

"Thanks, girls, for the delicious birthday dinner. I didn't expect you to make such a fuss over my fiftieth birthday." Milly gathered the last cake crumbs from her plate onto her fork.

"The fuss has just begun." Wendy picked up the plates and carried them to the kitchen.

"Ta-da!" Penny waved a package in front of her mother. "The best is yet to come," she said as Wendy plopped a tissue box on the table.

"What's that for?"

"You'll see."

As soon as she tore off the wrapping paper and opened to the first page of the scrapbook her daughters had made, she reached for a tissue.

"Where did you get these pictures?" Surprise pushed Milly's voice up an octave. "I thought the house fire when I was two and the second one when I was eleven destroyed all the childhood pictures my parents had." Milly looked from one smiling daughter to the other. "I know they did. I remember my mother crying about the loss."

"You're right, Mom, everything burned to the ground. But while we were regretting your misfortune, your aunt Phoebe decided to look in her attic." Penny smiled and passed her mother another tissue. "Sure enough, she found a few pictures from your childhood in her albums. She contacted some cousins and we came up with some more. Most of these pages are more recent, but we have one of you as a baby and one as a toddler."

"I don't remember

Tip

Where you only have a few pictures that represent the theme or time period, stickers can help convey the mood. Look for stickers that come with directions on the back, providing guidance on layering them to build attractive, meaningful scenes.

how my parents looked when they were that young." Milly studied the faces in the pictures showing her mother and father holding her.

"This one," Wendy said, pointing, "is a cousin's birthday party you attended."

"I remember that yellow dress. I loved how it swirled out when I twirled around. It burned in the fire when I was eleven."

Milly clasped the album to her. "You don't realize how precious pictures are until you lose them. They trigger a lot of memories you otherwise forget."

SPIRITUAL SNAPSHOTS

Memories are more precious than silver or gold.
Take care to plant good ones
by making time for family and friends.
A pictorial record allows us to keep our memories
alive. Psalm 103:2 instructs, "Bless the LORD,
O my soul, and forget not all his benefits."
The spiritual blessings God provides for us
are more important than gold.
They deserve first place in our memories.
If we ask, God will help us recognize our spiritual
benefits. When we do, we are less likely
to build that proverbial mountain
out of the molehills of our disappointments.

Pesky Brother

Who can understand his errors?
cleanse thou me from secret faults.
Psalm 19:12

"Boo!" Pepé slipped up behind Arturo, carrying a thick scrapbook. "Wanna see a secret?"

"Hello, where did you come from?" Arturo turned on the couch, trying not to look startled.

"I'm Pepé. I'm eight. How old are you?"

"I'm Arturo, and I'm twenty." Arturo held out his hand. "Glad to meet you. Ria said she had a younger brother."

"Ria's twenty-one. You're going on a date, right? She's still putting stuff on her face." Pepé chattered on, making it unnecessary for Arturo to answer.

The little boy grinned. "I'm sneaky like a fox. I like to sneak up on people. I saw you jump when I surprised you." Pepé hopped up and down. "I sneaked Mama's scrapbook out of the closet. Wanna see pictures of Ria when she was little?" Pepé plopped himself down beside Arturo and opened up the book.

On the page before Arturo, Ria stood with her

thumb in her mouth. She looked about two years old in the picture.

"She's cute." Arturo wasn't sure he should be looking at the family album without Ria present. Still, he relished the opportunity to find out more about the pretty brown-eyed girl from Tijuana he had met last week.

"She's not cute here." Pepé turned to a page in the back of the book. The snapshot showed Ria emerging from a tent, her eyes squinting after just waking up and her mouth wide in a yawn. "She's real ugly in the morning." Pepé flipped back toward the front of the scrapbook. "Here, she's in her pajamas. She didn't know how to button the back flap by herself yet."

Arturo had the grace to blush at the picture of Ria laughing over her shoulder at the camera, her chubby backside exposed by the dangling flap.

"Pepé, I'll get you!" Ria burst into the room and

snatched the album off Arturo's lap. The flame in her cheeks made the time she'd spent with the rouge pot unnecessary.

SPIRITUAL SNAPSHOTS

We treasure pictures that give us a look
into a person's personality.
When we look at the expression in someone's eyes,
the tilt of a mouth, we catch a glimpse
of the moment's emotions.
But scrapbooks can expose more than we wish,
as Ria found out.
God also records our actions and reactions.
We don't have any secrets before God.
He knows our innermost thoughts,
sees our every action, and hears our spoken words.
This sobering reality does not need to make us
cringe if, like the psalmist, we ask Him to forgive us
and cleanse us from our faults.
God views our life with the tenderness of a father
poring over the albums of his children.
Because of His great love for us,
He provided a means to escape His judgment.
We rejoice in His provision of Jesus Christ,
who offers us access to the mercy of God.

What's That?

A wise man will hear,
and will increase learning;
and a man of understanding shall
attain unto wise counsels.
PROVERBS 1:5

Grace and Gordon laid a scrapbook from their trip to Italy on the coffee table in front of their friends.

"It was a fabulous trip," Grace said, her eyes sparkling. "Look at the wonderful pictures I took." She turned to the first page, a picture of the Colosseum ruins.

"See how I snapped the picture right when a donkey cart carrying straw passed by? I had to wait a few minutes for the cart, but I thought it made the impression that we were back in ancient times."

"The tour guide told us about the red sand they used in the arena so the blood of people and animals wouldn't be as noticeable after a contest there," Gordon said.

"He did?" Grace looked at her husband with

surprise. "How fascinating. I don't remember him saying that."

"You were busy getting the donkey cart in the picture."

"Well, anyway, look at my great shots of the Forum. I loved the detail on this tumbled column, so I took a close-up."

Tip

Be sure to include interesting information in the journaling that accompanies your pictures.

"Those Acanthus leaves make it a Corinthian column," Gordon said. "The guide explained the difference between Corinthian, Ionic, and Doric columns."

"I don't remember him telling us about columns. I guess I should write Corinthian in the caption under my picture."

"You moved out of earshot to get the close-up of the Corinthian leaves."

"Did I take a picture of a Doric column?"

"Probably not. They're less ornate."

"I should have. My scrapbook would have been more educational." Grace clapped her hand over her mouth as she giggled. "I sure mixed up my priorities. I kept thinking about the scrapbook instead of learning from the guide first so I could make a better scrapbook second."

SPIRITUAL SNAPSHOTS

Pictures make more informative souvenirs
of a trip when they reflect what
we learned about the sites we saw.
We need information to make informed decisions.
Together, our decisions create a collage
that determines the impact of our lives.
If we seek counsel from godly people,
gain understanding from reading the Scriptures,
and keep our hearts open to hear the voice of God,
the pages of our lives will reflect wisdom.

Mining

But whoso shall offend one of these little ones
which believe in me, it were better for him
that a millstone were hanged about his neck,
and that he were drowned in the depth of the sea.
MATTHEW 18:6

"Where was this picture taken?" The chairman of the National Child Labor Committee questioned his staff photographer without taking his eyes off the picture on his desk. More than two dozen grimy-faced boys stared from the photograph. Their dirty faces were nearly indistinguishable from their black, worn clothing.

"In a coal mine in South Pellston, Pennsylvania," Lewis W. Hines answered.

"The boys look like they arranged themselves on these gritty boards and metal pipes in some kind of a pose for you, but there's not one smile in the bunch."

"You wouldn't smile either if you went into the mines before sunrise and didn't come up until after sunset." A nearby secretary shook her head.

"The boys' work in the mines is physically

exhausting and mentally deadening in its monotony," Mr. Hines said, gesturing to another picture.

The chairman nodded. "Look at the hopelessness in these girls' eyes. The North Carolina cotton mills are so poorly lit, you'd hardly know these girls work above ground. When we present your photographs to Congress, I expect to see a storm of favor for passing child labor laws. If not, then congressmen have hearts of stone."

From 1907 to 1917, Lewis Hines, driven by a passion to bring social change, photographed people working in miserable conditions. His work exposed the pathetic lives poor children lived. The passage of the first child labor laws in 1917 must have provided him with great satisfaction, even though courts declared them unconstitutional. It wasn't until 1938 that the Fair Labor Standard Act

Tip

Don't feel as if you have to clean your children up or comb their hair for snapshots. Pictures of disheveled children become precious with time and provide proof of the civilizing effect of growing up.

passed, providing the teeth needed to make child labor restrictions a reality. This time the courts upheld the law.

SPIRITUAL SNAPSHOTS

With or without pictures,
we want a sensitivity that desires
to rescue those around us from discouragement.
Even if the needs are immense,
we can become a vehicle to sprinkle God's
mercy on people with a hug, a favor,
or an encouraging conversation.
"He hath shewed thee,
O man, what is good;
and what doth the LORD require of thee,
but to do justly, and to love mercy,
and to walk humbly with thy God?" (Micah 6:8).

First Things First

A time to weep, and a time to laugh;
a time to mourn, and a time to dance.
ECCLESIASTES 3:4

"Oh, no! Our annual scrapbook retreat falls on Mother's Day weekend." Joan's disappointment carried over the telephone lines. "What does that do to our big cropping weekend?"

"Flushes it," Pam answered. At the silence from Joan, she went on. "No one looks forward more than I do to a weekend away to trim my photos and get my scrapbook caught up to date. But we can't arrange a big cropping weekend away from home when our families want to honor our motherhood."

"Not to mention honoring our own mothers," Joan said, regret heavy in her voice. "That particular weekend away would not be a good example about priorities for our children."

"Rats! All year I look forward to getting away from responsibilities to scrapbook and talk. Sometimes I even tell people about my faith in God at these events." Pam paused. "Guess that's not a good enough excuse. Showing our own children God's love is most important. It's good there's an annual day to make my kids remember they're glad I'm their mother. It's easy for them to take me for granted the rest of the year."

Tip

When you help children make their own attractive scrapbooks, they will have more patience with your hobby.

"Let's see if our church will let us do a sleepover for scrapbooking the weekend after Mother's Day." Joan's voice brightened.

"Good idea. There won't be any calendar conflicts planning this far ahead."

SPIRITUAL SNAPSHOTS

Our children notice our priorities.
If we want them to consider family important,
we must demonstrate its significance in our decisions.
A time away for refreshment may
well make a mother perform her role better,
but plan the break when it is best for the children.

9/11

Thou, which hast shewed me great and sore troubles, shalt quicken me again, and shalt bring me up again from the depths of the earth.
PSALM 71:20

Thanks, everyone, for coming." Sue stood in front of the group of twenty-nine women gathered in a church hall who had responded to a newspaper article. The purpose of this meeting was to make albums for the survivors of the September 11, 2001, terrorist attacks on the World Trade Center and the Pentagon.

"Did you notice how on TV the survivors of the bombing victims reached into boxes to find pictures?" Nods greeted Sue's observation. "Thanks to the compassion of one thoughtful woman and her leadership, tonight we are contributing to the movement she began. It's building into a huge effort."

Sue held up a five-inch by seven-inch photo album. "The goal is to supply lovely albums with patriotic decorations to everyone who lost a loved one in the tragedy of the 9/11 terrorist attacks." She then waved a sheaf of photocopied pages. "Every table has diagrams for arranging the stickers and borders on each page."

The women were already sorting and passing out the supplies and talking in hushed voices.

"Be sure to leave plenty of space in the center of each page for the families to mount their own pictures. When you are finished, fill a baggie with sticky dots for mounting pictures, enough page protectors for each page, and a black pen.

"The scrapbooks will be boxed and sent to families in Washington, D.C., New York, and Pennsylvania. Thanks again for caring enough to give up an evening." Sue busied herself passing through the tables to answer questions.

In the fall of 2001, large and small groups of women gathered in homes, churches, and civic buildings all across the United States. They decorated pages with flags, stars, and patriotic borders to create gifts aimed at providing grieving survivors an easy way to make memory albums about their loved ones.

Tip

An empty scrapbook makes a good baby or bridal shower gift.

The goal was to supply fifty-five thousand books and give one to each member of a victim's family. Women across the nation paid the price of the albums and supplies in a gesture of sympathy to the survivors. At the same time, the participants took comfort in finding something tangible they could do to alleviate their own grief and sense of helplessness.

SCRIPTURAL SNAPSHOTS

"He healeth the broken in heart,
and bindeth up their wounds" (Psalm 147:3).
God uses people to bring comfort.
Whether it's a casserole, personal visit,
or scrapbook, whenever we demonstrate
we care about a person's grief,
we are acting as God's messengers
to assist in the healing process.

Travel Dolls

Dear friend, you are faithful in what you are doing
for the brothers, even though they are strangers to you.
3 JOHN 5 NIV

Connie glanced around to make sure no curators were watching her in the museum gardens. With a quick tug she adjusted the striped skirt of her doll, balanced her in the crook of the marble statue's arm, and stepped back and snapped a picture. When she reached to retrieve her travel doll, a voice startled Connie and she nearly dropped the doll. The doll's straw hat fell to the ground.

"Bello," the native woman said as she stooped to retrieve the hat. "Bambola bello." She put the hat back on Connie's doll and fingered the doll's curls that hung out from under it.

"Thank you. The doll *is* beautiful." Connie smiled at the woman whose skirt reminded her of the outfit she had made for her doll, Lorelle, before she left the United States.

"Flowers make bambola picture bello." The signorina then took Connie's hand and led her to a bed of white lilies that formed a backdrop for the statue of a child, its arms reaching toward the sky.

"Si, beautiful, I mean, bello." Connie put Lorelle in the flowers and then, with a gentle hand, guided her new Italian friend into the picture.

After taking a photo, Connie took a small tract from her purse and handed it to the woman. On the front was a picture of her doll in Italian dress. Inside were a few simple words about Jesus written in Italian.

"Women in every country love bambola, si?" Connie gestured to her doll.

The Italian woman tucked the tract in her blouse and the two women waved to one another until Connie finally stepped around the stone wall and out of sight.

Tip

Each Christmas make a page of the toys the children receive. Place a Christmas theme scrapbook on a table as part of your holiday decorations.

"It worked again," Connie boasted to her husband when they met at a sidewalk cafe. "My travel doll makes friends wherever I go. Even though I can't speak the language, Lorelle helps relate to people in other countries." She positioned Lorelle on the wrought-iron table and took a picture before she sat down.

"People enjoy helping me pose my doll in places which make them proud of their country."

Travel dolls constitute a fascinating specialty of the doll industry. Women pack their dolls and an assortment of doll clothes when they go on a trip. Often the clothes are designed to match the area of the visit, such as cowgirl outfits for a trip to Wyoming. They place their dolls in the foreground of all the pictures they take. The doll owners make charming scrapbooks with the doll providing a unifying theme for the pages. Sometimes they send a copy of their pictures to the toy company, which, in turn, makes delightful scrapbooks full of dolls wearing a wide variety of outfits in exotic locations.

SPIRITUAL SNAPSHOTS

Connie used her travel doll to break down
cultural barriers and become
better acquainted wherever she traveled.
The universal appeal of dolls helped her make
friends with people she did not know.
The doll started many conversations,
leading to some opportunities to talk about Jesus.
Even at home, we can search for ways
to express interest in people.
When our lifestyle demonstrates God's love
and concern, we often gain opportunities
to speak about how good God is

and to contribute to a person's understanding of God. We bless our friends, new or old, by praying the apostle John's prayer in 3 John 2 (NIV): "Dear friend, I pray that you may enjoy good health and that all may go well with you, even as your soul is getting along well."

Short or Long

Whereas ye know not what shall be on the morrow.
For what is your life? It is even a vapour,
that appeareth for a little time,
and then vanisheth away.
JAMES 4:14

With a sweep of her arm, Diane sent a pile of snapshots tumbling from the kitchen table to the floor. Ginger, Harry's golden retriever, sat up from her nap at Diane's feet and shook off the ones that had landed on her back.

"Sorry, old girl." Diane stroked the dog's head.

Right after Harry died in an accident outside his college dormitory, the sight of his dog curled up on the floor caused Diane to wince in pain from the loss of her son. Now, seven years later, the dog which once followed her boy like a shadow was a comfort.

"Maybe I'm not ready to make a scrapbook about Harry's life yet, huh, Ginger?"

Diane couldn't focus on the gold-embossed album through her tears. "Why on earth did I buy a scrapbook, anyway?" She cupped Ginger's head in her hands.

The dog licked her face. "Okay, Ginger, I'll do it." With the retriever padding behind her, she went resolutely to the attic and hauled down a box labeled "Harry." After the funeral she had packed away the mementos of her son's life in a vain effort to "pack away" the pain of his death.

Opening the box, Diane laid the letters Harry earned playing soccer for his high school team on the floor. Ginger nuzzled the gold-edged C before plopping down on top of it. "Okay, girl, I'll ask the store how to put these thick things in a scrapbook."

Diane had almost forgotten how many art awards Harry received in school. She examined a picture taken of a china plate he'd entered in a contest. She put Harry's first-place ribbon for his work and a newspaper clipping about the reward on one side of a spread. She fastened the picture of the plate to the other side.

Tip

Be sure to date all your pictures. Once they are mounted on a scrapbook page, marking the date somewhere on the page makes it easier to see at a glance when the photo was taken.

She separated a bundle of newspaper clippings into two piles, one for his art achievements and one for the soccer games. By the time she made some pages showing Harry playing his guitar with friends, Diane surprised herself by finding comfort in the project. Picture after picture showed his face wide with smiles, often with an arm around a buddy.

By putting together the souvenirs of his life, she felt satisfaction sweep over her. His life had counted. Although short, Harry's life left an impact on his world. His years were few, but his joys were plentiful, his relationships happy, and his accomplishments satisfying. Her grief reduced by the scrapbook project, Diane finally released any remnants of resentment she had toward God because of her son's early death.

SPIRITUAL SNAPSHOTS

In light of eternity, life is a vapor.
Whether we live to ninety years or die in our youth,
our lifespan is but a moment in the perspective
of God. His plans for us may require years to
accomplish or may be realized in a short time.
Remember, God is in control of our lifespan.
That He knew the length of it before
we were born helps us keep our perspective.
Our responsibility is to use every day to the fullest.
When we lose loved ones, grateful memories
are an antidote for regrets about lost time.

Flashes of Insight

Let your light so shine before men,
that they may see your good works,
and glorify your Father which is in heaven.
MATTHEW 5:16

"Whoa. You didn't just take my picture, did you? My hair's a mess." Myra put her hands to her head.

"No one cares if your hairdo isn't perfect, Grandma. What I captured on camera was a sight never before seen." Mitchell waved his camera in the air as if he were displaying a trophy. "Grandma dancing a jig."

"Anything to cheer up a convalescent child, sick and tired of staying in bed." She gestured toward Eddie propped up against pillows, his rosy checks reflecting a combination of laughter and fever.

"How'd you sneak a camera in here?" Eddie asked.

Mitchell tucked the small camera in his coat pocket and pulled it out again.

"Where'd you get that little thing? Your grandpa's camera would never fit in a pocket, for goodness' sake.

It's huge." Grandma indicated a box the size of a loaf of bread with her hands.

"Join the modern world, Grandma. Since the War to End All Wars, Germany's putting science to good use. Ernest Leitz invented this miniature camera in 1924. It's 1929 and I decided it's time to get a new camera. This year, the camera companies came out with an electric flashbulb. Did you see the flash?"

"I did see a sudden flash of light. Why did that happen?"

"So I can take pictures indoors. Isn't that great? It beats carrying sick Eddie outdoors in order to have enough light to catch you dancing on film." He threw his arm over his head and mimicked Grandma's fancy footwork.

Tip

Read your camera's instructions about how to use the flash to eliminate backlight.

"You'll have a blurred picture, flash or no flash. I was moving too fast." Grandma swatted Mitchell with a napkin from Eddie's lunch tray.

"I hope it's not blurred. I'm sending this picture in to the newspaper for the community service award." Mitchell gave his grandmother a hug. "You ought to win, Grandma, because you're always taking dinner to some sick person or sewing clothes for poor babies or even dancing to cheer up Eddie. You are a bright light of hope, lots better than a flashbulb."

SPIRITUAL SNAPSHOTS

The ability to take pictures
with a flashbulb expanded opportunities
to preserve memories with snapshots.
After eliminating the need to pose
where there was plenty of light,
candid shots became popular.
Our lives are continuous candid moments
to the people around us.
The flashes of love others see when
they catch us in impromptu moments
show the love of Jesus.
God uses His light shining through us
to reveal His love to others.

Grandma's Legacy

*Behold, how good and how pleasant
it is for brethren to dwell
together in unity!*
PSALM 133:1

On Christmas Day eight grandchildren were mystified when they opened their gifts from Grandma. Instead of the usual hand-knit mittens, homemade doll clothes, and carefully hemmed handkerchiefs, each child found a spiral notebook like the kind they carried to school.

The adults, peeking over their children's shoulders, were the first to get excited about the contents of the notebooks. Soon the room was full of laughter as the family read stories recorded on the pages.

"Look, Mom, you still doodle on the edges of paper like you did when I was a kid," Kevin said, holding up his daughter's book.

"The doodles make pretty designs. Can I color them in?" his child asked.

"Of course, the scrapbook is for your enjoyment," Grandma said.

"Why is a picture of this movie star in my book?" Kirsten asked.

"I cut that picture out of *The Saturday Evening Post* because I thought it looked a lot like you," Grandma told her blond-haired granddaughter.

"Kirsten does resemble that star, doesn't she?" Kirsten's mother leaned over to look at the clipping.

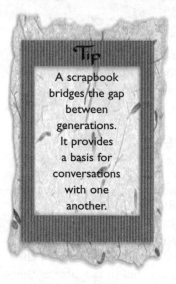

A scrapbook bridges the gap between generations. It provides a basis for conversations with one another.

"Where did you find this clipping? It's a gem." Harold read a sentence out of his boy's book.

"I've been keeping these notebooks for a while, and I don't remember where I found all the sayings. Sometimes I noted the source."

Claude burst out laughing. "Read the story on the second page. It tells about Grandpa tipping the swing over when he was courting Grandma."

"Yours is the only book with that story, Claude. You see, everyone's book is different." Grandma looked around the room at her family. "I made them different on purpose. You have to read them all to discover the complete family history. I wanted you to see them today so you'll know what I'm up to, but give them back to me at the end of the day because they aren't finished." She grinned. "I plan to keep on writing down appropriate Scriptures, family history, and advice in everyone's book until I die."

Grandma waved away the chorus of protest. "That's when I hope you'll want to read each other's books enough to keep up the family gatherings. You have to read them all to get a full picture of who I am. Regular family get-togethers is what I want as my legacy to you."

SPIRITUAL SNAPSHOTS

A close-knit family provides support, stability,
and joy for the family members.
The same is true for our church family.
When we take the time to become acquainted with
one another in our church and spend time together,
our church becomes a unit.
We understand our heavenly Father better
because He gives everyone a portion of revelation
of His nature, but He doesn't give any one person
the entire revelation. "Fulfil ye my joy,
that ye be likeminded, having the same love,
being of one accord, of one mind"
(Philippians 2:2).

Sentimental

And even the very hairs of your head are all numbered.
MATTHEW 10:30 NIV

When James turned to ask the waitress for more coffee, Lois inched her hand along the white tablecloth until it was over the toothpick James had just tucked under the edge of his plate. She felt a little silly. There were plenty of toothpicks to choose from in the small crystal holder in the center of the table. She'd probably put one of those in her purse, too, as a remembrance of this special night, but the wooden toothpick under James's plate was more sentimental because he had used it only minutes ago on his straight white teeth. Before he turned back, Lois secured her treasure and dropped it into her beaded evening purse.

When James invited her to dance, she paused to fold the white paper napkin with its scalloped edges and the hotel name embossed in gold.

"Come on. This is perfect music to dance the Lindy to," James said as he pulled her chair back.

"I just don't want the waitress to take my napkin

while we're gone. I want to save it for my scrapbook."
She didn't mind if James knew she saved the napkin,
but she was afraid he'd think her over the top if he
knew she collected his toothpicks as well. She didn't
have the nerve to tell him about the gum wrapper she
had squirreled away when they went out for an ice
cream last week.

All her friends told her you could lose a boyfriend
if you acted too crazy about him. She didn't want to
look like she was completely head over heels in love.
But she was. She hung onto his shoulder while they
danced just like she hung onto every word he said.
Each time he twirled
her around under his
arm, she smelled the
sweet scent of the gar-
denia corsage he brought
when he picked her up
for the Valentine's Day
dance. Before she went
to bed, she would flatten
it under a heavy dic-
tionary between two
pieces of wax paper.
With Scotch tape she'd
add it to the others in
her scrapbook, repre-
senting their year of
dating.

Tip

Scrapbook
supply stores
now sell tiny
acid-free plastic
sleeves to hold
memory tokens
on the pages of
your scrapbook.

She would search the February 15, 1955,
newspapers tomorrow and cut out the article about
the dance. She'd add that to the newspaper accounts

of James's YMCA baseball games last summer.

"He's the most wonderful thing that's ever happened to me," Lois countered whenever a girlfriend came over and laughed at her scrapbook. It was thick with such remembrances as dance cards, theater programs, ticket stubs from movies, and gift tags from presents he gave her for Christmas. Nothing was too small or trivial to mount in her book.

"James is the joy of my life, and I don't want to forget a single thing we did. I want a record of our dating life before we get married."

"I guess he's got to marry you to keep that book private," Lois's friend said, rolling her eyes.

Spiritual Snapshots

God's love for us is greater than any human love
we have ever experienced.
No concern in our lives is too small
for God to notice. He listens to every prayer
we utter and knows the ones we never say.
He gathers the experiences of our lives
with every bit of the care we gather
memorabilia to put in a scrapbook.
He is ready to joy over the glad happenings
and to comfort us in the sad times.
He delights to converse with us
and is ready to listen any time
we reach out to Him.

Hurricane Fran

A merry heart doeth good like a medicine:
but a broken spirit drieth the bones.
PROVERBS 17:22

He that is of a merry heart hath a continual feast.
PROVERBS 15:15

"Oh, great!" Fran flung the newspaper down and stomped to the kitchen. Maybe a cup of tea would prepare her for her husband's telephone call. Jerry was bound to phone as soon as he saw the daily newspaper at the office. After all the names he'd called her last night because she had knocked his wobbly pile of files onto the floor, and the night before when she broke the window pane by stumbling into it, pointed umbrella first, he wouldn't let this opportunity pass.

Why did the weather people have to pick my name for a hurricane? She reached for the offending paper while the water heated. HURRICANE FRAN, the headlines screamed in two-inch type. The subtitle told her people were already fleeing the Outer Banks islands to escape its fury. Some hurricanes fizzle into nothingness before they hit land. Why did her namesake have to bear high winds and promise great destruction? Jerry would taunt her about "her hurricane" the rest of her life.

Fluffy stretched from his nap and purred while making a figure eight around her legs.

"You won't call me names, will you, Fluffy?" Fran picked the cat up and tucked him under her arm while she dunked a tea bag in her cup. "Somebody loves me no matter how many mistakes I make."

"You'd think I'd get tough after five years of marriage and ridicule," Fran told Wanda when her best friend called. Wanda's jokes about her namesake storm didn't sting like Jerry's had. "It really isn't the storm, it's living with the constant attitude of criticism that threatens to unhinge me. I've made up my mind. I'm not going to let it get to me anymore. I know who I am in the eyes of God. If my husband doesn't have the grace to see my best side, I refuse to cower under the name-calling. I'm going to let it run off me like this rain runs off my windows."

Tip

If making a scrapbook to project humor, make sure all the comments are kind as well as funny. Leave out cutting, sarcastic humor.

"Good for you. It's about time you started

appreciating yourself." Even as she talked, Wanda was concocting a plan. "I'm not going to let you forget your resolve either."

Hurricane Fran blew through the area leaving behind a booming business for the tree surgeons, and twenty-four-hour days for the power company employees.

"At least I didn't kill anyone," Fran quipped at her birthday party a few weeks after the storm passed.

"I made you a reminder so that you don't let names penetrate your self-confidence ever again." Wanda said when Fran began to open her present. Wanda looked at Jerry, hoping he'd catch her point.

The black headline cut from the *Daily Press*— HURRICANE FRAN—announced the subject of the scrapbook on the title page. The party guests' laughter grew louder with each page Fran turned. Newspaper copy was paired with pictures of Fran for comic effect. One picture showed Fran waiting in line by a row of Port-a-Potties in a West Virginia rest stop. The headline about Hurricane Fran's rampage read, LOOKING FOR RELIEF. Another picture showed Fran's friend vacuuming. The newspaper clipping read, CLEANING UP AFTER FRAN.

By learning to laugh at herself instead of cringing, Fran demonstrated the truth of the biblical proverb, "A merry heart doeth good like a medicine." After this party, Jerry never saw the need to restrain himself from calling her names. But as Fran's laughter denied him the satisfaction of a reaction, the habit became less and less rewarding. Focusing on the humorous side of events, Fran blossomed with assurance in herself. Whenever she slipped back into believing the abuse, leafing through the hurricane scrapbook set her chuckling.

Spiritual Snapshots

A story circulated in newspapers and magazines
about a famous writer who responded to a diagnosis
of cancer by enclosing himself in a hotel room
with hours and hours of videotapes of
Abbott and Costello and Laurel and Hardy episodes.
The healing he experienced he attributed
to the hours of hearty laughter as much as
to medical treatment. While not recommending
laughter at the expense of medical aid,
we all know a good laugh lifts our spirits.
We can all attest to the truth of Proverbs 15:13:
"A merry heart maketh a cheerful countenance:
but by sorrow of the heart the spirit is broken."
Laughter helps our mental health.
It is a valuable gift for people to give one another.

Oops

If we confess our sins, he is faithful and just to forgive us
our sins, and to cleanse us from all unrighteousness.
1 JOHN 1:9

"M om! What are you doing?" Jason interrupted
Jean's troubled thoughts about her brother.

Seeing the expression on Jason's face didn't help
her forget her brother's troubles. When Jason was
angry, he looked just like her brother Robert. Only
Robert seemed to live in a constant state of aggravation these days. It was hard to say who was more
annoyed, Robert with his family or the family with
Robert.

Jean sighed and turned her attention to her nine
year old. "What?"

"Right there." Jason jabbed the snapshot she held
in her hand with his finger. "Look what you did! You
cut off the top of my head in my favorite picture,
wearing my White Sox hat." Jason grabbed at the
scissors his mother still held. "Why do you chop up
perfectly good pictures anyway?"

Jean held the scissors away. "Careful, Jason.

Scissors are dangerous."

"They sure are in your hands. I wanted my White Sox hat to show."

"I'm sorry, Jason. I made a mistake, but it can be fixed. I'll simply take the negative to the store and have another copy made and paste that one in instead."

"Don't cut it up this time."

Tip

Only cut up doubles for your scrapbook pages. Keep one copy whole in case you make a mistake.

"If I cut some of the pictures, more will fit on a page, and I can get rid of some of the stuff I didn't notice when I took the picture. For instance, that basket of laundry behind your hat gives the background a cluttered look."

"Mom!" There was the aggravation again. "I guess you didn't notice this either." Jason pointed to another picture already glued onto the scrapbook page.

Jean cringed. There, under a picture of Jason, she had written his brother Brad's name in elaborate calligraphy. "I'm sorry. I wasn't thinking."

"Maybe you think about Brad more than me. Is that why you labeled the picture with his name?"

"You know that isn't true. I made a mistake because I had Robert on my mind and the mistakes he's making with some of his choices."

"You'll mess up the page if you try to cross that

out and write my name under the picture."

"I can cover up the mistaken label with a sticker of a baseball bat and write your name under that. It'll fit right into the theme of the page and look like I meant it all along. I wish it were as easy to fix the mistakes Robert is making."

"Yeah, you mean the drugs and stuff?"

"I can't put a sticker over his actions and make them look okay." Jean reached out and pulled Jason onto her lap. "But I know who can cover mistakes no matter how bad they are. Jesus shed His blood on the cross so our sins can be forgiven." Jean gave Jason a squeeze. "Let's pray Robert will decide to ask Jesus to be his Savior and let Him be Lord of his life."

Together they prayed for Robert. With a playful punch, Jean added a prayer for Jason not to think she loved him less than Brad because of a mistake in her scrapbook.

SPIRITUAL SNAPSHOTS

A scrapbook mistake is minor compared to some
of the errors we make as we live day by day.
Our natural reactions and thoughts
don't always protect us from sin.
What a comfort we have knowing Jesus died for
our sins, and His blood is able to cover them up
and make us righteous in the sight of God!
God is able to take the mistakes of our lives
and fix them so we can still fit into His plan.
He will cover sins and rearrange our lives
so that we are profitable members of His Kingdom.

The Great Depression

"I have told you these things, so that in me you may have peace. In this world you will have trouble. But take heart! I have overcome the world."
JOHN 16:33 NIV

Bernice averted her face from the picture of a child in a ragged dress. The dress was much too large for the child, with one of the shoulders drooping halfway to her elbow. Her mother's ribs showed through her dress.

Eunice put more photos on Bernice's lap. "If you think those pictures Walker Evans took are bad, you should see the ones by Dorothea Lange."

Bernice cringed. "Do you think my sister is living in a log cabin as poorly constructed as this one?"

Eunice felt bad. "I forgot your sister and her husband left Boston for the West at the beginning of this Great Depression. I wanted you to see Dorothea Lange's pictures and those of Walker Evans because I think they show the spirit of our brave American people in hard times."

"I admired Earl's and Ruby's spirit when they lost

everything in the '29 market crash. They packed up their hungry children and headed West for less crowded land. Earl assumed they could grow their own food." Bernice's voice trembled as she pointed to a picture. "These kids don't look as if they've eaten a square meal in months."

"Look how proud this mother stands." Eunice searched for something encouraging to say. "Her ribs may show, but her spirit isn't broken."

"Let's collect food and clothing at church to send to people suffering in the terrible claws of our economy." Bernice stood up. "Maybe something will reach Ruby, if we only knew where she is." She swallowed hard. "At first she wrote, but before our mail could reach her, she moved again. Finally we didn't know where to address a letter. Maybe she stopped writing because she needs to spend their money on food, not postage."

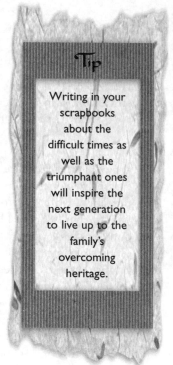

Tip

Writing in your scrapbooks about the difficult times as well as the triumphant ones will inspire the next generation to live up to the family's overcoming heritage.

"If your sister is struggling in rural America like

these people," Eunice said, tapping the pictures, "I know she's standing tall."

"I agree. Remember her favorite Bible verse, Deuteronomy 31:6: 'Be strong and of a good courage, fear not, nor be afraid of them: for the LORD thy God, he it is that doth go with thee; he will not fail thee, nor forsake thee.' "

Her own courage strengthened, Bernice grabbed her pocketbook. "Let's go talk to the minister about a clothing drive. May I keep one of these pictures for my commonplace book? It will ensure my prayers for my sister are fervent."

SCRIPTURAL SNAPSHOTS

America was built by people who sacrificed
to secure a better future for their children.
From the early settlers to the pioneers
who traveled West by covered wagon,
people built their courage on God's Word.
From the suffering of the Great Depression
to September 11, 2001, brave people have trusted
God to overcome. Pictures tucked in formal
and personal scrapbooks bear testimony to
the courage of our great nation.
The foundation of great courage is trusting
God who gave His Son to overcome the world.
We, too, can stand tall in suffering
because God is with us.

The Diamond Room

Jesus saith unto them, "Come and dine."
And none of the disciples durst ask him,
Who art thou? knowing that it was the Lord.
JOHN 21:12

"Why do you call this a dining room?" Tom surveyed the room where his wife sat at the table alternating different patterned papers on the page before her. He leaned against the doorway, his eyes twinkling in amusement. "There is way too much paper scattered all over the dining room table to sit down and have a meal here."

"Are you making fun of my hobby?" Marta grinned back at him. "I'll have you know, it's efficient to have all my scrapbook supplies laid out, ready to pick up at a moment's notice. By leaving everything out, I can come in here and lay out a few stickers when I can snatch a moment." Marta waved a sheet of decorations at her husband. "If I put it all away every time I stop, it takes that much longer to get ready, and I need to have a big chunk of time to make the effort worthwhile. You do the same thing with your workbench in the garage. You like to keep your tools out and ready to grab."

"Yeah, but I don't claim I'm going to feed you a meal from my workbench."

He picked up a handful of stickers from the sideboard. "A sticker buffet awaiting your pleasure." Tom bowed with an arm behind his back and then sprinkled the stickers over the buffet.

Tip

Scrapbooks appreciate in emotional value as the years pass. Money is a poor substitute for good memories.

"Don't mess up my order. There's order in my mess." Marta scooped the stickers up and dropped them into a drawer of the hutch.

"How much money does all this represent?" Tom was enjoying himself. "You must have a small fortune in all this paper." Tom's gesture took in the entire room. "I think we should change the name of this room from the dining room to the diamond room."

Marta joined his laughter. "Just think of this as my greens fee and my tackle box. Only my supplies don't cost nearly as much as your hobbies."

"You got me." Tom picked up some paper that had fallen on the floor. "Never let it be said I don't appreciate our diamond room."

Spiritual Snapshots

As we appreciate the texture of
some special paper or lovely design,
God enjoys us, His creations, even more.
Every facet of our lives is important to Him.
He always desires and enjoys our companionship.
He always has a banquet laid out for us to enjoy
with Him. He never retracts His invitation to
"come and dine." If we dine at the table He sets
before us, we are truly dining in a "diamond room."

A New Way

But now, by dying to what once bound us, we have been released from the law so that we serve in the new way of the Spirit, and not in the old way of the written code.
ROMANS 7:6 NIV

"Mom, I can't wait for you to see the scrapbook from my Mozambique mission trip. You'll love the pictures of the children's meetings." Betty's enthusiasm came through the phone lines.

"I'm eager also, but the doctor said I can't travel as far as Pennsylvania for three months. I didn't think you were free to come here right away, either." Rosaline tried to tone down the longing in her voice.

"You're right about my coming there, but you'll be able to see my scrapbook before the week is out."

"Do you think it's wise to mail a scrapbook?" Betty's mother asked. "I'll never forget when your dad's pictures of his brother's wedding got lost in the mail."

"I don't plan to mail it."

"Then I'm confused. Is your sister Joyce coming to visit you and then bringing it back with her?"

"No, Mom, it's new technology. I'm putting my pictures and my comments on a compact disc. I'll send it to Joyce over the Internet, and you can see the whole thing on her computer when you go to Joyce's house for Sunday dinner."

"You can do that?" Rosaline shook her head in wonder.

"If you ever decide to take us kids up on our offer to get you a computer, I'll send you your own compact disc and you can play it over and over as much as you want."

Tip

Insure scrapbooks if you must mail them. Keep copies of the pictures in case of loss.

"I'm too old a fossil to learn about all these whizbang inventions," Rosaline said, dismissing the idea of owning a computer.

After Sunday dinner, Rosaline sat at her daughter's computer and looked at the scenes of Mozambique. "I can't believe how good these pictures are. You say they came over a wire, like the telephone? I never understood the telephone, let alone this marvel."

"I don't understand how it works either, Mom," Joyce said as she scrolled down to another scene. "You don't have to understand everything to use a computer. You use the telephone, and you just said you don't understand it."

"Look how happy Betty looks crowding those

three children onto her lap! Do you think she's found her calling and will go to Mozambique for the long term?"

"She'll be far away if she does." Joyce sighed.

"Maybe I should try to use a computer to stay in touch with her. Do you think an old woman like me could learn?"

"Sure you can," Joyce said, patting her back. "I'll teach you. Bets and all the rest of your kids will send you plenty of pictures of your grandkids. Won't it be fun to keep up to date with all their events without waiting for the mail?"

SPIRITUAL SNAPSHOTS

Modern technology drives change in our society
at a fast pace. Although at times we feel breathless
trying to keep up with the changes,
none of these inventions surprises God.
He provided the inspiration for every creative
act humankind has performed,
whether people give Him glory or not.
He also provides us with His Holy Spirit,
who instructs us and builds us up
in our understanding of God. When we ask,
God sends His Holy Spirit to help us with
our daily life in our fast-paced world.

Immortality

These things have I written unto you
that believe on the name of the Son of God;
that ye may know that ye have eternal life,
and that ye may believe on the name
of the Son of God.
1 JOHN 5:13

"I've used great paper for my scrapbook—it's supposed to last four hundred years. The salesperson said this ink I bought won't deteriorate the paper either." Liz held up the scrapbook full of baby pictures. "Johnny's scrapbook will last for centuries."

"How long will the paper the pictures were developed on last?" Gwen asked.

"I checked that out, too, and changed to a company that uses archival paper guaranteed to last."

"Who's going to enforce the guarantee? You won't be here in four hundred years to complain." Nicole reached for the book.

"In four hundred years who's going to care?" Gwen shook her head. "Even Johnny's grandchildren will be long gone. His descendants will be in the fifteenth generation by then and up to their ears in family memorabilia."

"Historians care." Liz tried to keep the hurt from showing on her face but the pitch of her voice betrayed her.

"I'm sorry. You've made a wonderful scrapbook." Nicole held up a picture. "Johnny's a precious little boy, and God will always care about him. I can see why you want to preserve all these neat facial expressions of your baby. He's your treasure."

"I'll bet his grandchildren will want to know about him," Liz said, pressing her lips together. "I wish someone had used archival stuff when they put together the scrapbook of my grandmother and her brothers. There are holes in many pictures where the ink ate into the paper. My mother's childhood pictures are so yellow and fading, they're hard to see. I wish someone would take the time to fix them so they won't deteriorate anymore."

"That's the catch, taking the time." Creases furrowed Gwen's forehead. "Who has time to go back over old books? I barely have enough time to do what I should each day to feed my kids and make sure they have clean clothes."

"That's just the point." Liz pointed to her book. "Do it right the first time, and some future generation won't be looking at it with regret."

"How far into the future will generations bother to look at the scrapbook at all?" Gwen picked up Liz's picture. "We're all just dust and to dust we return. I don't want to spend too much time living in the past. My hope is to live each day fully."

"I'm sorry, Liz, we aren't making fun of your careful records." Nicole tried to soothe her friend. "You're right. Historians do learn a lot about the past from ordinary people's journals and old pictures."

"Yeah, they'll learn how much trash a single family dwelling can hold when they excavate the site of my house a millennium from now." Gwen made a wry face.

Liz laughed with the others. "I guess everyone kind of longs to live forever. Since we know we can't, we want to leave something that will live on after us."

"How true," Nicole said as she picked up her friend's Bible. "The only way to immortality is through knowing God's only Son. I guess the best way to leave something behind is to help others know God's Son, and to train our precious treasures like Johnny to hold fast to the teachings of this book. That way God's ways will go on in the lives of our descendants."

Tip

Ask your film developer if he or she uses archival paper.

SPIRITUAL SNAPSHOTS

Scrapbooks are a valued source of
information about bygone generations,
and often treasured by those who follow.
The best everlasting inheritance comes
from leading people to Jesus Christ.
When a person receives Jesus as Lord,
His covenant lasts forever. "
"He hath remembered his covenant for ever,
the word which he commanded
to a thousand generations" (Psalm105:8).
And we are guaranteed the inheritance will keep.
" 'Lay not up for yourselves treasures upon earth,
where moth and rust doth corrupt,
and where thieves break through and steal' "
(Matthew 6:19).

Unto All the World

"And the King shall answer and say unto them,
Verily I say unto you, Inasmuch as ye have done it
unto one of the least of these my brethren,
ye have done it unto me."
MATTHEW 25:40

Poor soul!" Marie sat in the waiting room of a cranial-facial surgeon's office holding a scrapbook on her lap. The book lay open to a picture of a woman with a tumor that engulfed half her face and hung down past her shoulder.

"But look at the next page," her daughter, Becca, said, flipping it over. A series of snapshots showed the results of a succession of surgeries, ending in the final portrait of an attractive woman.

"Don't you think she looks pretty?" Clarise, Marie's granddaughter, asked.

"Amazing. Dr. M is fantastic."

"He is. No one in this woman's remote village could help her, and she couldn't have afforded the procedure if there had been a facial surgeon there. Dr. M said the woman hiked for two days from her little village to see him."

Becca added, "Can you imagine walking so far with such a heavy tumor?"

Clarise told the stories of other patients pictured in the scrapbook. Everybody displayed big smiles after Dr. M used his remarkable skill to repair their deformities.

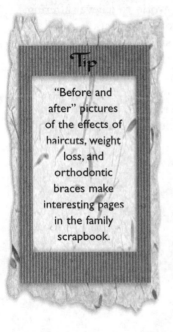

Tip

"Before and after" pictures of the effects of haircuts, weight loss, and orthodontic braces make interesting pages in the family scrapbook.

"If he can make these people look good, you are in good hands, Clarise. Your beautiful forehead will still look lovely after he removes your tumor."

"See why I wanted you to come, Mom?" Becca grinned at her mother. "I knew this pre-op visit would give you peace about Clarise."

"Looks like you found a great doctor."

"Wait until you meet him. You can tell his driving motivation is to help. He wouldn't travel all over the world to fix people for free if he weren't full of compassion. He serves God."

SPIRITUAL SNAPSHOTS

Dr. M is a great inspiration.
His selfless service to humankind takes him
to primitive parts of the world to relieve suffering,
without hope of remuneration.
We may not have the skills of a great surgeon,
and we may not be able to afford to travel around
the world, but we can use the unique abilities God
gives us. No matter how insignificant we view
our talents, we can use them to bless the people
who populate our little corner of the world.

Inspirational Library

Beautiful purse/pocket-size editions of Christian classics bound in flexible leatherette. These books make thoughtful gifts for everyone on your list, including yourself!

When I'm on My Knees　　The highly popular collection of devotional thoughts on prayer, especially for women.
　　Flexible Leatherette. $4.97

The Bible Promise Book　　Over 1,000 promises from God's Word arranged by topic. What does God promise about matters like: Anger, Illness, Jealousy, Love, Money, Old Age, and Mercy? Find out in this book!
　　Flexible Leatherette. $3.97

Daily Wisdom for Women　　A daily devotional for women seeking biblical wisdom to apply to their lives. Scripture taken from the New American Standard Version of the Bible.
　　Flexible Leatherette. $4.97

My Daily Prayer Journal　　Each page is dated and features a Scripture verse and ample room for you to record your thoughts, prayers, and praises. One page for each day of the year.
　　Flexible Leatherette. $4.97

Available wherever books are sold.
Or order from:

Barbour Publishing, Inc.
P.O. Box 719
Uhrichsville, OH 44683
www.barbourbooks.com

If you order by mail, add $2.00 to your order for shipping.
Prices are subject to change without notice.